I0126289

# AN UNLIKELY SOCIAL JUSTICE WARRIOR

Ani Zonneveld

# AN UNLIKELY SOCIAL JUSTICE WARRIOR

## Making My Life Count as a Muslim Feminist

## Activism and Social Movement Studies

Collection Editor

**R. Anna Hayward**

LPp

First published in 2025 by Lived Places Publishing

All rights reserved. No part of this publication may be reproduced, stored in a retrieval system, or transmitted in any form or by any means, electronic, mechanical, photocopying, recording, or otherwise, without prior permission in writing from the publisher.

No part of this book may be used or reproduced in any manner for the purpose of training artificial intelligence technologies or systems. In accordance with Article 4(3) of the Digital Single Market Directive 2019/790, Lived Places Publishing expressly reserves this work from the text and data mining exception.

The author and editor have made every effort to ensure the accuracy of the information contained in this publication but assume no responsibility for any errors, inaccuracies, inconsistencies, or omissions. Likewise, every effort has been made to contact copyright holders. If any copyright material has been reproduced unwittingly and without permission, the publisher will gladly receive information enabling them to rectify any error or omission in subsequent editions.

Copyright © 2025 Lived Places Publishing

British Library Cataloguing in Publication Data
A CIP record for this book is available from the British Library.

ISBN: 9781917566995 (hbk)
ISBN: 9781917566452 (pbk)
ISBN: 9781917566476 (ePDF)
ISBN: 9781917566469 (ePUB)

The right of Ani Zonneveld to be identified as the Author of this work has been asserted by them in accordance with the Copyright, Design and Patents Act 1988.

Cover design by Fiachra McCarthy
Book design by Rachel Trolove of Twin Trail Design
Typeset by Newgen Publishing, UK

Lived Places Publishing
P.O. Box 1845
47 Echo Avenue
Miller Place, NY 11764

www.livedplacespublishing.com

"Some Muslims force people to fit into a box called Islam whereas I look at Islam as lifting people out of their boxes."- Ani Zonneveld

# Abstract

In 1981, 18-year-old Ani landed alone in the middle of rural Illinois from Kuala Lumpur—adrift in an unfamiliar landscape of corn fields, cows, and Caucasians. As a privileged daughter of an accomplished Malaysian politician and diplomat, Ani shares her journey overcoming the common thread of patriarchy, sexism, and prejudice at the intersections of music, politics, religion, and human rights, which exposes inconvenient truths and lifting us out of tribalism and into allyship with each other.

## Key words

Feminist, religion, patriarchy, conflict, LGBTQ+, women's rights, interfaith, colonialism, lived experiences, allyship

# Acknowledgments

My oldest brother Azahari did an oil painting of me titled "The Warrior", depicting a woman with a *kris*, a Malay dagger, strapped to her back. He always saw me as an *avant garde* warrior, recognizing what has become core to my identity before I saw it in myself. Azahari was my protector, holding up the pitchfork between our conservative family members and myself, giving me the space I needed to let my free spirit flourish. He passed away January 30, 2024 leaving a hole in my heart.

I can never thank my parents enough for all their offerings to me—the many life lessons, the privileged upbringing that allowed us to live in so many countries immersed in the cultures of the world, and along the way, the gift in the diversity of friends, which has shaped my inclusive worldview.

My life has been enriched by so many friendships, but there are a few good folks in particular who have been there for me, lifting me up. Among those are Karima Bennoune, Maliha Khan, Frej Fenniche, Marilyn Wyatt, Rabbi Jim Kaufman, and Kevin Jennings, who after Azahari, has been my most ardent champion and mentor.

This book would not have been written in the way it was had it not been for the work of Sherine Elbanhawy, who dedicated time into poking holes in my initial writings and nurtured me into emoting more, and in allowing myself to be vulnerable.

My husband, Arthur—my steadfast anchor—has supported me through every journey that my free-spirited nature has led me on—from being a songwriter to becoming a human-rights advocate. He ensures that, as I soar, I remain grounded in reality. And my daughter, Jasmine—now my greatest teacher—keeps me connected to the dreams and aspirations of Generation Z, and, from that prism, encouraging me to remain authentic to who I am.

# Contents

# Introduction

One of my primary motivators for writing this book was my experience guest lecturing in classes on ethics at the Institute of Social Ethics at the University of Lucerne, and in several classes on Islam and human rights at University of California, Los Angeles (UCLA) and Yale. In these experiences, I have found that I am able to pique the interest of students by helping them to connect the theory that they are learning with the lived experiences, and the impact it has on people's lives through the work I do.

To connect with you emotionally, this book is filled with stories and anecdotes of experiences that I've lived through, which I hope will help you see the world in a more inclusive prism. I prioritize this inclusivity because, far too often, we humans take sides simply because of a shared identity. We've been raised to protect our own kind, be it along political, racial, religious, or national lines. Regardless of whether it's in the music business, the field of social justice and human rights, or in religious communities, it is remarkable how tribal we humans are. We get defensive of our kind even when our kind have acted criminally. It is this nature that results in conflicts at the global scale. How we see each other, and how we treat each other, impacts the environment we live in, the politicians we elect, and policies we enable.

Weaving in and out of this book are stories that will challenge stereotypes and defy the divisiveness that consumes us. In these stories, I explain what's in my head and what's in my heart. I drop names and call out hypocrites, while lifting up those who value and work toward the collective well-being of all of humanity. I give examples of cutting down patriarchal structures at their knees by using alternative thinking and applicable practices that I hope will inspire you to create inclusive cultures—particularly those who are entrapped in intense patriarchal communities. Above all, these stories point out how to build trust to advance human rights, not just for yourself, but, just as importantly, for others as well.

Before I go any further, let me first explain the title of the book.

In the human rights space I work in, often around people of faith, the word feminist is usually frowned upon. It has been misunderstood to mean anti-men or men-hating women. It was therefore important to include the term "feminist" in the title of this book to explain that, although I identify with the values of feminism, that is the belief in and advocacy of the political, economic, and social equality of the sexes, I also acknowledge that there are different approaches and tones in the ways in which feminists conduct themselves. Mine is just one example.

It was also important to include the word "Muslim" alongside "feminist", as my advocacy work is deeply anchored in the spiritual teachings of Islam. Many secular activists, and especially secular Muslims will take issue with this, as they see the terms feminists and Muslim together as an oxymoron. At the launching of one of the programs I spearhead, #ImamsForShe in Tunisia, I was, as expected, challenged by the religious right. But a secular feminist also stood up and said "how dare you put Islam and feminist in the same sentence!"

For those Muslims and non-Muslims who see feminism as an exclusively western and agnostic value, I challenge them with the examples of the Prophet Muhammad's own actions— appointments of a woman as an *imam* and as leaders of the early Muslim community. He was the first Muslim feminist.

Sexism and patriarchy are dominant infrastructures that benefit a select few. Reshaping that infrastructure and the centuries-old mindset that accompanies it requires collective engagement and action from us all, working in allyship with one another. Regardless of whether you're a Muslim or not, spiritual or not, I hope you will learn from my life experiences of being continuously challenged and still actively choosing to do better, not just for yourself, but for those who are in need. For it is only when we lift each other up collectively that we can finally dismantle the walls of inequality and oppression built by the patriarchy.

# Learning objectives

Through a series of chapters, Ani shares her personal experiences, challenges, and insights as she navigates her identity as a Muslim woman—challenging patriarchal norms, and championing human rights. The book covers topics such as music, sexism, patriarchy, Islam, interfaith marriages, and LGBTQ+, with the aim of highlighting how:

1.  Power dynamics shaping the narrative we consume has us pitched against each other.
2.  Political and religious authorities work together to bolster their power through divide-and-conquer tactics.
3.  Individuals can establish their own alternative social and cultural structures outside of the patriarchal and sexist systems.
4.  To think strategically and to look at the big picture.
5.  To learn how to connect dots, and how to work in allyship with unlikely partners toward a shared vision.

# 1
# Who am I?

"Ani, I'm sending you off to college. You will NOT do music, and you WILL do something useful with your life!"

Those were my father's commands.

At the age of 18, I was sent off alone to college in Illinois. Upon arriving in Chicago, I hopped onto a small propeller plane bound for Moline, Illinois. Seated beside me during this short flight was an elderly white woman, and we engaged in a genuinely pleasant conversation. As we were about to part ways, she posed an unexpected question, asking, "You seem like a very nice young lady; what church do you go to?" Caught off guard, I hesitated for a moment before responding, "I'm Muslim." To my surprise, she replied, "Well, I have never heard of that church before!"

I was taken aback by her response, as I was surrounded by friends from diverse races and faiths as a diplomat's child. For a total of 16 years, I lived in Germany, Egypt, and India, an experience that taught me to see people for who they are, not by the color of their skin, or what their parents did for a living.

My first experience as a minority was at the age of five at the British elementary school in Bonn, West Germany. The whole school would gather in the assembly hall, and every morning, before the principal spoke, we would say the Christian Lord's Prayer. After a few mornings, I confided in my mother about me praying to Jesus. "What do I do?" I asked. To which my mother responded, "Just replace Jesus with Allah and you're fine. We're all praying to the same God."

My mother's simple wisdom, urging me to make this simple adjustment in the Lord's Prayer became a guiding principle, reinforcing the notion that, beneath the surface, if we prayed, we all pray to the same higher power.

In this context, the realization that someone had never encountered the term "Muslim" left me astonished, and a tinge of fear began to seep in. I thought, "Where in heavens did my father send me to!"

When deciding on which university to attend, I staunchly declined my father's suggestion of the University of Arkansas with a rebuttal, "Dad, considering the history of the South, I'm not going to Arkansas!" Despite my father's well-read nature, his first choice was probably rooted in the idea that Arkansas is probably a boring enough of a place and would keep me out of trouble. My reservations, however, were rooted in the grim imagery of a history lesson in high school about racial violence and oppression at the British School in New Delhi. This perception culminated in the haunting image of a black man hanging from a tree, etched into my memory. It is within this backdrop that my initial interaction with a native of Illinois left me with a disquieting feeling.

In September 1981, I arrived at the airport in Moline, Illinois— the smallest I had ever encountered as an 18-year-old who had been traveling since the age of two. With an oversized brown suitcase, a carry-on bag, a modest amount of cash, and the contact details of a Monmouth College representative— who was supposed to pick me up—I faced the possibility of an uncertain night if they didn't arrive. Keep in mind, this was 1981—a time void of cell phones or smartphones to scout nearby hotels, and I had no credit card to rely on. After enduring a grueling journey from Kuala Lumpur to Hong Kong, from Hong Kong to Narita, then Narita to Chicago, and finally Chicago to Moline, I was simply exhausted. Needless to say, my relief was palpable when the representative materialized. After collecting my suitcase, a motherly-looking woman with a warm smile approached me, asking if I was Zuriani Osman. I guess, given I was the only brown person off the plane, I was easy to spot! Her presence made me feel secure and I allowed myself to relax, the weariness to take over, and in the car ride to Monmouth through the endless countryside landscape of cornfields and cows grazing, lulling me into a deep sleep.

During my inaugural semester in the United States, amidst the crisp fall air of Monmouth, a flier at the student union building caught my attention—an announcement of a guest speaker, Louis Farrakhan from the Nation of Islam. This confused me a bit. The old lady on the plane had said she had never heard of "Muslim", and yet here was a Muslim speaker at this rural town. Needless to say, I was very intrigued, as I had never heard of a Nation of Islam, and in my younger days, one could describe my personality as uber-ly "FOMO", or fear of missing out. I made my way to the venue early, securing a spot in the last row, in an aisle seat close to the exit door, just in case I needed to escape.

As the room filled, I observed the women—clad in all-white attire, white *hijab*, exuding elegance, beauty, and a serene aura. Their dignified demeanor reminded me of the way my mother carried herself minus the hijab, back straight, chin up, but unlike these women, my mum always wore a smile. Following suit, the men entered, donning sharp suits and bow ties, equally radiating dignity, standing tall and proud. The men didn't smile either, nor did they greet the audience. I noticed that right away, as we Malays almost always carried a smile. The room was packed, with folks standing along the sides of the room. Then Louis Farrakhan walked in with his entourage, and he started to speak. With the dignified appearances of the Nation of Islam attendees and the way they dressed and carried themselves, my mind was prepared for a speech that was equally dignified, uplifting, positive, and memorable. But when Farrakhan opened his mouth, I was so taken aback by his words. I could not believe what I was hearing.

Farrakhan's speech delved into racist and prejudicial commentary about people of other races and religions, particularly White people and Jews. He smiled, but it was accompanied by a deceptive tone, and his choice of words was simply vile. After many decades, I don't remember his exact words, but the emotional memory stuck with me. Disgust welled up within me, an unfamiliar emotion. What was it that I was listening to? How could this man of faith, a Muslim, speak of others in such a manner? Raised in an environment void of hate in the name of religion, where my parents had never expressed prejudice toward other races, religions, or sexualities, this experience was so alien to me that I didn't even know what to call it (Photo: Ani's parents).

**Figure 1:** Ani's parents, 1970

At eighteen, and although "fresh off the boat," so to speak, I knew about slavery and Jim Crow, but I knew nothing about the Nation of Islam, an organization now designated as a hate group by the Southern Poverty Law Center. Over the years, I have come to learn that America is home to so many hate organizations that it needs an independent entity such as the Southern Poverty Law Center to monitor and identify such groups, starting with the plethora of White-supremacist organizations.

Now, many years wiser, I understand the reasons for the founding of the Nation of Islam, its historical context, its roots in racial struggles, and the quest for self-empowerment among African Americans. I understood it better, especially after 9/11, in how unsafe and oppressive the environment was for American Muslims as a result of the American government's "war on terror" in other words, its anti-Muslim policies. With the war on Gaza on October 7, 2023, the outbreak of anti-Muslim hate has taken on another meaning, starting with the murder of six-year-old Palestinian boy Wadea Al Fayoume, who was stabbed 26 times. Other acts of hate crimes have since been perpetrated, but authorities have been reluctant to call them as such. Families of Palestinian Americans killed by Israel Defence Forces in Occupied Palestine receive only lip service from the State Department about "getting to the bottom of it", whereas Israeli families (not Americans) killed by Hamas get to meet high level American officials multiple times. The preferential treatment is blatantly discriminatory, and I question the loyalty of our own government officials.

What American Muslims are experiencing is institutional racism. African Americans and the Indigenous people of the Americas have endured this for centuries and continue to experience it. Therefore yes, I get why the Nation of Islam came to be. Yet, I remain unconvinced that self-empowerment necessitates demonizing others. Demonizing others is an act of small-mindedness.

As I learned from a young age, the world isn't just Black and White, as there is a whole spectrum of colors in between. Through life's lessons, I've come to understand that hate, prejudice, and love resides in most of us, regardless of the color of our skin. While it is easy to succumb to hate and prejudice, it is really hard work to overcome them and tap into the expansive space of love. That is the human struggle.

*** 

I remember how 9/11 marked a pivotal moment in how being Muslim automatically meant "representing" a community, imposed on us in the form of a negative collective identity, discriminated against, and assumed to belonging to the terrorist tribe unless proven otherwise. Quite different from the American legal mantra "innocent until proven guilty".

Representing your community and your culture was a responsibility I carried growing up. I know that feeling too well. It is burdensome. From an early age, as a person of color and a minority living in Germany, I was taught to present myself in a dignified manner. Everything, from my manner of speech to my choice of clothing, carried the weight of the message: "You are a representative of Malaysia, and your words and actions reflect on our nation." Open-toed footwear and jeans were not permitted; instead, closed-toed sandals, slacks, or dresses were the norm. As a result, my wardrobe underwent meticulous curation. Even when my hair cascaded down to my waist, it was consistently maintained—combed, braided, or secured in a ponytail. The responsibility of grooming me or styling my appearance fell to my mother or caregivers, all with the aim of molding me into a paragon of "respectability."

As a child, I had no choice but to go with the flow, but as a teenager, "respectability" felt suffocating. Being hard-wired that way was understandable for the role I was dictated to play in protecting the country's reputation, but it was definitely not helpful in the doggy dog world of the music business in Los Angeles.

It was in this new American setting that I made a concerted effort to shed the obligation to "represent." It was hard, as it was not just about living up to your own individual identity but the balance of being part of a community without allowing the community to dictate the parameters of who they want you to be. Finding this healthy balance is a struggle for many immigrants, but for me, letting go of this responsibility to represent became a necessity—for my own well-being, for my own liberation.

The hyphenation of my identity to include American and Muslim took root.

And so, when 9/11 forced Muslims to "represent", it was in the spirit of independence and fueled by anger that I felt compelled to insert an alternative narrative to the dominant ultra-alpha male narrative, in the form of a female voice, through my music. It drove me to write, produce, and perform an entire album's worth of material centered on promoting egalitarian values, human rights, self-empowerment, and a poignant reminder of women's roles in Islam. It was the first time I shyly uncurled my middle finger to an authority. My first expression of independence and resistance. It felt good.

Crafting songs became a skill, but it started out as innate as breathing, an untrained instinct ingrained within me. In 2004, I took the step of releasing the album "Ummah Wake Up," (Ani/Zonneveld, 2003) using this creative outlet to voice my thoughts and forge an artistic form of resistance against patriarchy. My objective was to address a wider audience, including individuals like the elderly lady I had conversed with during my journey to Moline, Illinois, when I was eighteen. Through my music, I aimed to offer a musical and educational channel, countering misinformation and fostering a deeper understanding among the public. It was my small contribution to dispelling stereotypes and prejudice of Muslims and Islam.

It was through music and songs that I allowed myself to express freely. Music was my gateway. Over time, this permission became the new norm, enabling me to unwire what my parents had wired me to be, slowly discarding the old wires and replacing them with fiber cables. Through music, I learned to be me.

*** 

Being far from home and independent at 18 years old taught me to survive. After graduating from college and moving to Los Angeles, hard knocks and "paying my dues" were quite the reality check from my very privileged and sheltered upbringing. The music business was brutal. It was racist and still is sexist, and as an outsider without the connections to open doors for you, it was a very difficult time of my life, but I learned from it.

Trying to pitch a song or a music project and getting rejected was nothing new to me. As a songwriter, I would write, program the music in my home studio, and work in recording studios to lay down the vocals, and "live" instrumentation, and mixing.

It cost about $1,000 to record a song which entailed paying for singers and musicians, and studio time. Writing and producing songs was an investment in your resources, with no clear return on that investment, but producing the product was how you pitched your writing and production skills to publishers, artists, and other songwriters. It was these songs that helped you get into meetings for them to "check you out" before they would want to consider investing their time in meeting with you. It was the equivalent to the creators who pitch their products in "Shark Tank" today. You had to have a product to sell. As the saying goes, "show me what you got!"

By the time I had written and produced my first Islamic pop album at 42-years-old, I had already been a 15-year veteran songwriter and producer in the music industry in Los Angeles, with 40 songs published worldwide, and a few awards under my belt. I could write and produce in my sleep, and I knew how the distribution of music works.

With my album "Ummah Wake Up" on hand, the next step was to get it distributed and get publicity for the product and sales. The most obvious distributor, I thought, would be to Muslim retail stores, and there were quite a few of them, many distributing Islamic religious songs called "Nasheed". In Malaysia, *Nasheeds* were sung by male and female artists. Gender and music in general was not an issue, but apparently, in America, Islam has regressed such that women were, and still are, barred from singing, particularly in front of male audiences.

My calls to many online retailers failed to get any response— instead, I received the typical silent treatment, no different from the music industry. This silent treatment puzzled me, as I thought, post 9/11, as a vilified segment of the American population, we were all united in our Muslim identity and sticking up for each other. Shouldn't my Muslim community appreciate this counter-narrative? Little did I know I was wading into a marsh pit of sexism and patriarchy, no better than the secular music industry.

After many calls to retailers, I was finally able to get through to a Los Angeles Muslim online retailer, *Islamicity*. This company distributed a lot of religious content, including music, but evidently, only that of male performers. That was in 2004.

"Don't get me wrong Ani, we love your music," he said apologetically, "we listen to it all day at the office, but we just can't sell it. Our shoppers will boycott us."

"Why?" I ask.

"Well, first, you are a female singer, and a female voice is *aurat*, (to be covered), it's sexual. Secondly, you used all the musical instrumentation in your production, and during Prophet Muhammad's time, there was only the *dumbek* percussion, so therefore, only a drum is permissible as a musical accompaniment."

First off, I don't consider my singing style sexual at all. It is far from Britney Spears, Shakira, or Beyonce's sexual lyrics and gyrating hips. Secondly, this man should get off the phone and off the internet if he's restricting the use of a musical instrument to that of the 700s.

The hypocrisy is jarring.

I am taking up space to explain the nuances and context for the censorship of women's voices because it always starts with the voice, but it never ends there. This mindset is anchored in sexism and patriarchy, and it needs to be named.

I was raised in a very traditional Muslim family and culture, so this sexism in the Muslim music industry in America has nothing to do with respectability, appearance, or religion. It is censorship, which is a pervasive, regressive mindset among many Muslim organizations. This mindset is also deeply embedded in conservative Muslim societies—where women, by default, sit in the back of the room, and where it is the men's voices and opinions that dominate a space. Or, in the case of Afghan women, their voice and role in society are completely erased.

I remember an open call in 2005 for performers for a music festival, MuslimFest, organized by Sound Vision in Chicago, clearly and publicly stating, "Female performers need not apply." The festival organizers protested the *Globe and Mail* article with an open letter, but proof is in the pudding. There were no female musical performers.

This gender discrimination was, and still is, clearly evident at most co-ed Muslim events and conferences. Go to any mosque or fundraising event, and you will not see an adult woman performing a song. It has improved in that women can now perform spoken word and poetry. Even at the 2023 Islamic Society of North America Convention, only male musical performers were listed as providing entertainment. According to their logic, male singers are permitted, as apparently women do not get sexually aroused by male performers. This contradicts the reality, though, when I see Muslim girls in *hijabs* screaming for male singers at concerts. Somehow, this is not sexual attraction. The Islamic Society of North America (ISNA) is an umbrella organization consisting of thousands of mosques, which sets the tone for Islam in America. It is driven by a Wahhabi interpretation of Islam, the version that predates Saudi Arabia's Prince Muhammad bin Salman's version. Wahhabism, like most conservative branches of religion, look a lot like each other. It is very hierarchical and patriarchal.

To counter this fixation of a female singing voice, a group of progressive Muslims organized a musical event, and I was invited to perform at a one-day conference in Chicago, across the street from where ISNA was holding its annual conference. Some ISNA attendees went out of their way to hold up placards condemning us to hell. This expression of religion is what I call "zealots playing God."

There was one glimmer of hope to secure a distribution deal when a young male marketing officer at Yusuf Islam's (Cat Stevens) production company in London "Mountain of Light" reached out to me for a copy of my CD "Ummah Wake Up" for consideration for a distribution deal. Being a huge Cat Stevens fan, I was so thrilled at the request! But after many months of silence, the CD I sent was returned with a letter politely declining to digitally distribute the album claiming lack of funding.

On their website, the label distributed all-male groups, all of the artists sang acapella and accompanied with a *dumbek* only. It was evident that the label was gender-biased, stemming from a misogynistic and regressive interpretation of Islam, expressed and implemented in a business model. All the artists they had signed were men and even after claiming there was no funding for me, they continued to sign not one, but three all-male vocal groups. The sexist and patriarchal thread continues...

The website and company no longer exist, and I wished there had been such a thing as "taking a screenshot" for my own record keeping. Again, I was discriminated against. To be at the receiving end from your so-called co-religious left me feeling spiritually "homeless" and without a community I wanted to belong to.

For those not in the music industry, or those only familiar with digital downloads, an online distribution of a finished product was easy money. There were no out-of-pocket expenses of producing the content, such as booking studio time, hiring musicians and producers to record new material, as a newly signed artist would necessitate.

Distribution expenses usually include getting the CDs manufactured, marketing, the cost of storage space, and the labor of sticking the CD in the envelope and postage, expenses that would be covered by the retail price paid by the consumer, marked up by at least by 50 per cent or more. Like I said, easy money.

If I was getting turned down for financial reasons, or because the music was awful, then I would not have taken issue with it. The censorship of a female singing voice in the name of religion is absurd. What is astonishing is that the Muslim world outside the United States is rich with female singers including religious-themed genres by Uyghurs, Kazakh, and Kyryyz women, who accompany their singing with percussion and lutes, or the Sufi qawwali singers, a tradition dating back to the thirteenth century. And here's the kicker, nowhere in the Qur'an is music or the female singing voice prohibited.

These negative experiences I went through in the name of Islam, and by male patriarchs, are examples of men's "foot on our necks" to quote the late US Supreme Court Judge, Ruth Bader Ginsburg. These patriarchs are the same ones who talk a good talk in interfaith settings of how the Qur'an gave rights to women, which is true, but they don't practice it. And here's the best part. The very same company, *Islamicity* that declined to distribute my music in Los Angeles (LA) invited me to present their organization by performing at an interfaith event. This fake inclusive front is still a facade.

From my experiences, patriarchy is embedded in all cultures, religions, and races, and dominates the world regardless of what occupation or line of work you find yourself in.

I have experienced patriarchy in all its forms, from those closest to me and from afar. Patriarchy manifested itself in my mother, the music business, the world of religion, and even in interactions with human rights advocates. The hierarchical structure of patriarchy, including the women who support that structure, could be found in society's expression of caste systems, colorism, racism, sexism, and most prolifically, in religion.

The interpretation of "Islam" as we know it today is alien to me. It was not in the manner my father raised me, and is the doing of Wahhabism, the newly formed Saudi interpretation, "new" as in 250 years old in the context of Islam's 1,400-year-old history. This version is incredibly dogmatic, void of the right to think freely. It is cruel, misogynistic, suffocating, and as we have witnessed, even at times justifies violence. It is this version of Islam that has permeated Muslims across the world, mainstreamed by petrodollars, and has now become the dominant version, displacing the multitude of Muslim cultures around the world into a homogenous one. In short, it is Wahabbi cultural imperialism.

In 2022, as if in an epiphany, Saudi's Prince Salman claims *hijabs* are not necessary in Islam, women are allowed to drive, and music, and films are now permissible. This is an attempt to create a new image, erase, and sports-wash their imperial reality. For those who have experienced it hands-on, like the many human rights defenders I know who are sitting in jail, it is the same facade I saw with American Muslim organizations, but on another level.

Juxtapose this worldwide Wahhabi reality with the Muslim culture I was raised in, with Malay as my heritage, where my mother drove, where there were women professionals at all levels of society, from judges to the fishmonger calling out their fish at the top of their lungs. In a multi-religious and multi-ethnic Malaysia, we would greet and celebrate in each other's religious festivities. We would sometimes dress in each other's traditional attires as a way to show acceptance and appreciation of other traditions. As Malaysians, it was never considered "cultural appropriation," as it has become in America, nor was there a power element involved. Wearing each other's cultural attire was an endearing way of accepting and celebrating with others.

On the other end of the spectrum, Muslim social media forums are filled with questions such as, "Can I wish my Christian neighbors 'Merry Christmas' or will I go to hell?" These questions are so absurd in the twenty-first century, as if they are reinventing the wheel of coexistence when Muslim societies have always been multi-religious and multiethnic, and where intermarriages were not a taboo.

The term *aurat* is the bane of Muslim women. *Aurat* in Arabic means, the parts of your body that need to be covered. The older generation of Muslim women didn't wear headscarves or *hijab*, not even in Saudi Arabia. And even if Saudi Arabia has reversed its Wabbhist tendencies, their negative influence is deeply entrenched in Muslim societies that will take another generation or two to do away with because we are still told to cover our hair, our skin, and even our voice. It was this second-class treatment of women, the demeaning of a woman's worth that I experienced, of my God-given right to express myself freely that I faced the weighted decision of reassessing my Muslim identity.

# 2
# Pure intent

As a songwriter and producer in the music business, I lived my life equivalent to the "don't ask, don't tell" climate that LGBTQ+ people lived through—or, in some cases, still live through. Closeted and fearful to being "outed" as a Muslim and the repercussions that may come out of that.

I was always told to live my life with intent and purpose. However, I couldn't truly embrace my authentic self and reach my full potential while keeping an aspect of my identity, my Muslim heritage, a secret. The fact that my name is Zuriani Zonneveld and not an obvious Muslim name, made it easier to live incognito. The real challenge wasn't dealing with unwelcome inquiries; it was confronting and defining whether I wanted to still be a Muslim, and if so, what being a Muslim actually mean. This became an identity crisis, and in short, the aftermath of 9/11 compelled me to face it head-on.

Whether I was going to remain a Muslim or not, I knew I had to prepare myself for the inevitable barrage of difficult questions, a period of tests, and potential discrimination. I recognized the need to become well-versed in Islam in order to justify why I am a Muslim or why I left the faith. I delved into its theology, aiming to equip myself with the knowledge to respond to any inquiries in a clear, rational, and compassionate manner. Regardless of how challenging the questions might be, my goal was to be prepared.

As an example, there is a verse in the Quran 4:34, infamously known as the "wife-beating" verse. Members of the anti-Muslim camp, usually made up of ex-Muslims, the Christian Right, and Zionists, eager to scorn Muslims and Islam often use this verse to demonize the community. Frankly, I had no idea there was such a verse, and I was supposed to be Muslim!

The Arabic word *daraba* in this infamous verse has many meanings, one of which is "to walk away", which is what Prophet Muhammad did in an argument he had with his wife. In American lingo, we call it "time out". However, what has become mainstream is the translation "to beat," therefore giving permission for the husband to beat the wife should she disobey, giving false religious credence to domestic violence.

This is one verse of many that I needed to sift through, and in later chapters, I will delve deeper into others and the counter-narratives I use in my work. For so many years, my parents had always chided me for not thinking deeply enough before opening my talkative mouth. Well, decades later, I finally heeded them when I started the journey of critically relearning Islam.

I am a spiritual human being, I find connection to the Creator in nature, through music, and through service. I dislike the term religious because of the inherent patriarchal and discriminatory nature of its dogma and those who adhere to that dogma. I am not religious, and my ritual is serving humanity.

As I embarked on ascertaining whether I wanted to be a Muslim or not, I set clear intentions for myself: "If my path leads me away from Islam, so be it; if it draws me closer to Islam, then so be it."

Identity is a complex and central aspect of our humanity. It can either foster security or breed insecurity. Many of the abuses and violence I encounter in my current human-rights work stem from these insecurities. Whether within the family unit, between spouses, within religious institutions, supremacist ideologies, or in politics, insecurities often manifest as negative forms of power.

Reflecting on that moment decades ago when I hesitated to answer "I'm a Muslim" to the elderly woman in Illinois, I've often wondered why I hesitated. Now, years later, I realize that because I was living far away from my parents, I was subconsciously embarking on a journey of self-discovery. However, genuine self-discovery requires being a critical reader and thinker—with the luxury of time to contemplate. Yes, it is a scary inward journey, but one that is necessary if we are to grow.

As I unstitched the Muslim identity I was raised on, I came to realize that much of what defines us as "Muslim" and our religious practices isn't necessarily rooted in the Quran. Many distortions and the misplacement of our values can be traced back to interpretations crafted by men centuries ago. These interpretations, enshrined as Sharia law, embodied patriarchal and misogynistic, self-serving versions sold to lay Muslims as God's laws, which much of the Muslim world has latched onto as absolute "truth." This falsehood that Sharia law is God's law begins to shape perceptions from a young age, usurping our right to read, to think critically, and to think freely. It limits, insists, and imposes the belief that the path to heaven lies solely in obedience— obedience to the designated religious authorities. For women, this obedience extends to their husbands, which, of course, is all about control.

Muslim-majority nations and governments, often in collaboration with religious authorities on their payroll, dictate the definition of being a Muslim. They do so in the name of God, or Allah, while paradoxically undermining the very principles in the Quran that grant individuals the right to think freely, express themselves, and connect directly with the divine. These governments prescribe a specific version of Islam that their citizens must adhere to. If you're literate enough, they control the accessibility of what is available to read, and if you're daring enough to articulate your thoughts, you may be whipped and jailed for defying "God's law."

Islam al-Behairy, a very popular television preacher was jailed in 2015 by the court, under the government of Egypt of President Sisi for "contempt of religion". Al-Behairy was challenging the authenticity of various *hadiths*—a debate that needed to be had. *Hadiths* are a collection of writings compiled one to two hundred years after the passing of Prophet Muhammad, attributing them to his sayings and actions.

Many Muslim-majority countries and their religious tools position themselves as religious guardians while often engaging in corruption and violence, conveniently cloaked in the name of Islam. And unfortunately, the very supporters that prop up these dictators are the Western governments that claim to stand for freedom of expression, and for freedom of religion and belief. This hypocrisy is obvious to the people on the streets in Muslim societies, especially in the Middle East, but somehow oblivious to these Western governments. This hypocrisy is made even more evident by the anti-war protests of the Israeli war on Gaza at American colleges, and the unflinching support of Israel by Western governments regardless of its many human rights violations, UN conventions that all these member States have signed on to uphold.

The powerful dictators and their corrupt religious leaders in the Muslim world are not unlike figures such as Donald Trump in the American political landscape, who have instrumentalized the Christian Right for his political ends. Much like in the Muslim world, power lured the Christian Right into moral corruption. We also see the utility of Orthodox Judaism in Israel giving itself special privileges over Reform Judaism and secularism, and of Zionism cloaked in Judaism as a tool of oppression of Muslim and Christian Palestinians. They are all morally corrupt and have given God a bad rap.

In many Islamic institutions, the prevailing theology is one that often elevates males above females, perpetuating a sense of male superiority. Even in so-called "moderate" mosques, teachings brand menstruating women as "impure," leading to restrictions of prayer and of touching the Quran. False beliefs insist that God won't accept prayers if led by a woman, that men are the "guardians" of women, and that being gay and Muslim are incompatible. A menstruating woman is sometimes viewed as a sexual object, thus leading to prohibitions against her singing or delivering sermons before men out of fear of sexually arousing them. If this seems familiar, it is because we've seen how the Taliban took this theology to a brutal level.

In more radical mosques and cultures, imams may advocate for a husband's right to physically harm their wives, propagate intolerance toward other faiths as well as Muslims who don't adhere to their definition of Islam such as liberal and progressive Muslims. In some cases, these teachings go so far as to condemn homosexuals to hell and, in extreme instances, endorse capital punishment against them.

The root of these theological perspectives remains consistent; the only difference is the severity of the scorn and punishment. What I found particularly enlightening was the realization that these teachings are not rooted in the Quran itself but rather in the *hadith*. What is even more intriguing is how some individuals who identify as devout Muslims employ these contentious texts to validate their interpretation of "Islam," while simultaneously, those with a negative disposition towards Islam, also known as Muslim-haters or Islamophobes, merely replicate and disseminate these texts as evidence that "Islam opposes democracy and human rights." One cannot help noting the irony that those who enthusiastically share these contentious texts often harbor not only anti-Muslim sentiments but also exhibit similar biases, such as misogyny, homophobia, and prejudice against those who do not conform to their specific identity. In essence, they are, in many ways, two sides of the same coin.

If you take a closer look at the Quran, it emphasizes justice a whopping 52 times, emphasizing mercy, compassion, and doing good for humanity. Plus, it encourages us to care for all of God's creations, from animals to the environment. So, it makes you wonder if Muslims have been approaching our faith practices in reverse gear. Instead of selfishly racking up prayer points to secure a spot in heaven, shouldn't it be about serving others?

This is where my hat's off to atheists. The ones who are generous and donate to noble causes do it because they genuinely care about making a difference, not to earn brownie points with the Almighty. That's sincerity at its purest form.

The unraveling of my Muslim identity marked just the first leg of my journey. I never expected there would be a second act. But as the old identity faded away, a new one started taking shape. This one had purpose, and it ignited a passion within me that has led me to live a life I could have never predicted, one that's incredibly fulfilling.

With my new understanding of the Quran, it was evident that patriarchy reigned over the religious leaders at my mosque. To stay would have made me a hypocrite. The easiest decision was to quit the mosque.

The uncurling of my middle finger was less shy and more assertive.

*** 

I consider myself lucky to have been able to find my own identity and to live it. My Uncle Mak Bakar wasn't so lucky.

Through my 16 years of living abroad in Germany, Egypt, and India, my uncle Bakar, whom we called Mak Bakar, lived and traveled with us as our chef. He was my mother's oldest brother and was the one who prepared our meals. When dinner was being served, he would hit the Malay gong, filling the house with its low ring lingering in the air long enough for procrastinators.

For the family, Mak Bakar's daily cooking was usually our local Malay food of *kurma, curries,* stir fried vegetables, and desserts such as *bubur kacang, curry puffs,* and other savories.

He was definitely a good cook! His signature dish was the *chicken kurma,* which, until today, reminds me of him. On occasions when my parents were hosting dignitaries for a sit-down dinner or a glamorous reception, such as on Malaysia's Independence Day (from the British), we would hire extra hands for a French service or hors d'oeuvres served by uniformed waiters. But otherwise, his cooking was of the Kedah Malay cuisine, which was our culture.

Mak Bakar had a sway in his hips when he walked, and when he was tasked with teaching me and other Malaysian girls traditional Malay dances, those hips swung at an even larger degree.

His hands were feminine in how he twirled them in the traditional *tarian lilin* (candle dance). He taught us to twirl our hands holding a small plate in each hand, a candle burning, and our rings tapped in rhythm on the plate. The only time I saw him smile was when he was dancing.

Apart from attending his dance classes, I had very little inter-action with him for the span of 16 years, except when I'd ask for food. Our conversations never delved deep, and there seemed to be an invisible barrier between us, which I couldn't comprehend until many years later.

One day, when I was around ten years old, we were living in Cairo, and I decided to venture into his living quarters, which stood separate from the main house. He sat outside, engrossed in a contemplative moment, cigarette in hand, wearing that distant expression that often accompanies smokers lost in their thoughts. My sudden appearance took him by surprise.

"What are you doing here?"

"Just exploring," I said.

He shooed me away, "Go, go, you are not allowed to be here. You need to go back."

Throughout my upbringing, I rarely set foot in the kitchen, except to assist my mother during her experiments in bak-ing, usually in the early afternoons when Mak Bakar took his breaks. Despite sharing the same roof for years, he never joined our family at the formal dining table; his role was strictly confined to serving. Occasionally, I would dine at the kitchen table when Malaysian students were visiting us, and at times, he would join us.

It wasn't until well into adulthood, long after I had grasped the concept of homosexuality, that I approached my oldest brother, Azahari, with a question about Mak Bakar.

"Was he gay?"

He broke into a broad smile and confirmed, "Yes, he was!"

I now understood the presence of that invisible wall and his comment that I wasn't "allowed" to come to his living space.

Mak Bakar passed away many decades ago, and I never had the opportunity to thank him for feeding me and my family. I would like him to have known that I would have accepted his sexual identity. Looking back, I regret not making more of an effort to get to know him.

The ability to "find oneself" and openly express oneself is indeed a privilege. I never realized it until I embarked on my own journey of self-discovery. As a secure adult comfortable in my identity, I often reflect on how sad it is that my uncle carried his gay identity with him to his grave.

Coming out as a Muslim has been, and continues to be, a challenging experience, but it's also incredibly liberating. Helping others in discovering their true selves remains one of the most rewarding aspects of my work and life. When people can openly embrace their true selves, they tend to be happier and more fulfilled, and being at peace with oneself is foundational to contributing to a more peaceful world.

As Bobby McFerrin sang, "Don't worry, be happy," it's worth noting that genuine happiness often requires a profound journey of self-discovery, and the fierce desire to be true to yourself. Sadly, for too many people, being true to oneself is a luxury they cannot afford.

# 3
# "Girls can't do that!"

Even as pragmatic as my upbringing was, I didn't escape the dehumanizing narrative that girls grow up with. It was my mother, not my father, who was the mild promoter of misogynistic beliefs in the name of Islam. Living in New Delhi as a teenager, around 13 years old, I used to learn the phrases and the pronunciations of the call to prayer or the *azan*. One day, though, in the confines of my bedroom I was practicing the *azan* with my bedroom door ajar. Upon overhearing me, my mother rushed to my room with fear in her eyes and panic in her voice and commanded, "Stop, stop, stop!"

"Why?" I asked, taken aback by her frantic gestures.

"Because you are a girl! Women are not allowed to do the *azan*!"

In my head, I retorted, "That's whack!" I remember that day vividly, a moment that shaped who I became, which I learned much later is a feminist.

Fast forward, in adulthood I've been invited to do many Islamic calls to prayer, including at our community prayer spaces and at the launching of an inclusive mosque in Berlin. But, the most memorable, and the most iconic, moment was doing so at the Gay Men's Chorus Los Angeles' summer concert at the Disney Concert Hall in 2017! (Photo: GayMensChorus LA 2017). With that one moment, I shattered the assumption that all Muslims are homophobic, and that love for humanity reigns. I have the Gay Men's Chorus music director, Dr Joe Nadeau, to thank for his kind and thoughtful invitation.

**Figure 2:** GayMensChorus LA 2017

As the Malaysian ambassador, on certain occasions, my parents would organize lavish receptions at our residence or at the Embassy. Our guests included dignitaries such as Morarji Desai of India and Prime Minister Indira Gandhi, both of whom I had the privilege of meeting in person. There were also more intimate dinners at our home, like the one with Mrs Jehan Sadat whom we hosted in 1972. As a side note, apparently inviting the wife of the sitting president for dinner was a trend my mother started in Cairo. It prompted other ambassadors' wives to follow suit.

For the dinner with Mrs Sadat, we also invited government officials and their wives, as well as the Malaysian diplomatic staff and their spouses. Instead of subjecting me to playing the piano for entertainment, a task I dreaded, they opted for a different start to the evening—a woman reciting the Quran. Like many other events that I wasn't formally invited to, I would tip toe a few steps down from the second floor and lay as flat as I could on one step to watch and listen in.

The recitation of the Quranic verses was melodic and endearing, and the Egyptian guests sat unmoved, but their hearts were moved, because according to my mother, tears rolled down some cheeks. Just like in the oral tradition of old, and even in the new, the voice, whether male or female, has a spiritual element to it that no instrument can ever mark up to.

And that is why my mother's reaction to my call to prayer confused me. It was as if in a professional and official setting there was one standard, and another for the family. It was all the more confusing when I later learned that my father chaired Malaysia's International Quran Reading Competition in 1964, which included a women's category with men and women in the audience.

The common denominator between some Muslim cultures and the music business in America is sexism. As of 2023, female music producers made up only 6.3 per cent of the industry. Back when I was in the business—from the mid-1980s to 2007, it was 2 per cent. I was one of the odd ones doing programming, arrangements, and mixing, not exactly the girl thing to do. This was men's territory. Women were often pigeonholed into the role of lyricists, melody makers, and singers.

I recall an experience in where I received a phone call, "Hello Zuriani. Mr. Mancini heard your tracks, and he would like to meet with you." Needless to say, I was super excited!

The music tracks I pitched were a fusion of rock, funk, and ethnic beats, long before Beyonce's song "Baby girl."

Upon arrival, I was taken to a room, "Mr. Mancini will be right with you!"

When he entered, Mr. Mancini looked around, expecting there to be someone else with me. "You did these tracks?" he asked, pressing play on the cassette player.

"Yes!"

"I mean you programmed and played the instruments?"

"Ummm, yeah!" unable to hide my irritation and my non-existing poker face.

Needless to say, the conversation ended up being very short and uncomfortable. That meeting didn't get me anywhere.

Clearly, Mr. Mancini assumed that a man had programmed the tracks, and it was hard for him to wrap his head around the fact that a square-looking woman could have played and produced such music. I didn't fit the image that people in the music industry expected. I wore my hair naturally black, in soft waves, and dressed more appropriately for an office setting rather than the typical look of torn jeans, colored spiky hair, a visible tattoo or two, or a piercing or a nose ring. In other words, I was still dressing up like a "proper diplomat" which sent the message "there was no way this 'normal' looking woman could have produced such a ballsy track!"

I had to unlearn the way I was raised to dress growing up, and many decades later, I learned to "dress the part", only to realize that once you've reached a certain threshold, in the entertainment business, nobody cares how you dress because "you've arrived!" It is all very confusing and liberating at the same time.

I really was a fish out of water, and with no mentor to hold my hand. I was and still am musical, although I just don't fit into the American music culture. The arts, in general, are not necessarily a space where faith is welcomed. Often extremely secular, and even anti-Muslim or anti-Islam—Muslims, particularly those in the music business, that want to advance in the industry, tend to run a mile away from their Muslim identity. I could probably write a mini-book on the hang-ups of Muslims in the arts, the gatekeepers they keep, the homophobic types, the egalitarian types, and those who just don't give a damn about anything but themselves.

Racism was another issue that I struggled with. In the late 1980s through the early 2000s, struggling to fit in, people were very cliquish, mostly into their own race group. This was during a time when music was very racially divided, when Black artists were automatically streamed into the R&B charts, the alternative genre were for White rockers, and it was only when you got to the top of those segregated charts that your song could cross over to the pop chart, which is where the money is. If you were a Black lead singer in a rock band or a Black country singer, the music industry had a really tough time marketing you and overcoming the racial barriers, at least that was how they thought and operated. Darius Rucker of Hootie and the Blowfish wrote about this, and on Charley Pride's first country album, his face was not on the cover. Music Television (MTV) didn't play videos of any Black artists until famous White rockers raised the issue. Finally, "Walk This Way" a song by Run-D.M.C. featuring Aerosmith music video broke the racial barrier down, which opened the door for Michael Jackson's videos to completely dominate MTV.

It is important to note the allyship for Black artists received from Aerosmith and other prominent White artists. Allyship is important. If we all support each other's causes in the plethora of social issues, we can be more effective and successful in lifting each other up in our humanity.

I am not Black, White, Latino, or Jewish, I am Southeast Asian and not Korean, Chinese, or Japanese, collectively labeled as East Asian, which is what most Americans expect when you say Asian. When one is part of a tribe, there is a communal support of shared understanding, challenges, and an inherent sense of having each other's back. Since Southeast Asians in the industry were insignificant, I did not have the benefit of that camaraderie, but then, I never sought them out either.

When people speak of prejudice and racism, in the American context, it is almost always assumed to be White versus Black, but as a person of neither of these two races, I have been excluded or discriminated against by all races or groups of people, White, Black, Chinese, Jewish, and from Muslims too. I think it is important to name this.

And now, for a little bit of history. In the late 1980s, songwriters sent our music or tracks and song demos, or samples, by mail on an analogue tape called cassettes. Then, in the 1990s, technology advanced to CDs. Nowadays, songwriters, producers, and artists send their music out digitally over the internet instead of having to stand in line at the post office. Imagine that!

During those pre-internet days, connecting with industry folks was a challenge. The way an unknown transplant like me could build relationships was by attending songwriting workshops and song-pitching sessions with publishers, which you had to pay to attend. In these workshops, surrounded with other songwriters, all of us were trying to get our "first cut." Getting "a cut" meant having a song placed on a record to be released.

When we were in our twenties, I remember how my bestfriend and I would sometimes go to jazz or R&B bars and approach musicians about possibly collaborating. It was our way of networking with musicians who were usually songwriters as well. The friends I tagged along with were usually the types who "dressed the part." Remember, I was terrible at that. My friend had a lot more self-confidence and natural street smarts than I did, which helped start many conversations, something I was also not very good at doing. Once a conversation got started, I would be introduced and included. In my younger days, I didn't have the confidence of inserting myself unless spoken to, while nowadays, I see my silent presence more as self-confidence with no desire to waste my breath on small talk.

In the realm of conversations, I've always found my stride in more active settings—be it strolling through nature on a hike or engaging in a spirited game of ping-pong. One particular memory that stands out is the time I challenged the rapper

LL Cool J to a ping-pong match in the recreational room of a recording studio.

It was an unexpected and delightful encounter, marked by the high-pitched sound of the ball smashing the table and the excitement of competition. As the game unfolded, laughter echoed through the room—LL Cool J's friends cheering on and teasing him for losing to me. There, in that friendly match, the thrill of the game went beyond the paddles and the score; it was a reminder of "don't judge the book by its cover", and that girls can play a mean game of ping-pong too!

I was myself in that 30-minute game, my comfort zone, harking back to my teenage years of playing against boys older than me and beating them.

Being an unestablished, single woman in the music industry is complicated. It makes you vulnerable, with land mines to avoid. Getting hit on was common, just another day at work, which young women, especially in the arts, still endure to this day. During those days, I would often wear a fake wedding band on my finger in an effort to throw off any hint of "single and available." Part of being a creative person is letting your guard down, fully expressing yourself, and allowing vulnerabilities to come through. It is also these vulnerabilities that allow for miss-signals. Finding the right balance between expressing yourself through a song and working with male collaborators, while at the same time, having the walls up enough so as to not give the wrong signals or to be taken advantage of, was a constant process. How high those walls should be depended on each co-writer I was working with, and every individual was different. It was, of course, much more liberating to work with men, who were simply talented professionals and yet friendly, a rare combination.

Being vulnerable is also a constant in my human rights work. In order to move people to come to your side, to learn about my work, to feel empathy means sharing stories about my experiences, the funny, the sad, the challenges, and the inspirational ones. Sharing vulnerabilities do put your emotions to bare, and there are times when people just step on them, gaslight me, "mansplaining" or even "womansplaining".

Being vulnerable and authentic are qualities that expose us, but whether it be in the music business or human rights work, that is what makes the human connection memorable. To negotiate that space between being vulnerable and being victimized is a tricky business. Men have to negotiate this space too, and I know several men whose careers were sabotaged or destroyed for sharing a vulnerable moment with the wrong male colleagues.

For women, though, after the #MeToo movement, it is evident that being vulnerable can expose oneself beyond emotional exposure to something more nefarious.

Interestingly, breaking into the music industry as a programmer and producer in a society with more traditional patriarchal norms, such as Malaysia, proved to be a comparatively smoother journey than in the United States or Europe. Part of this ease stemmed from the novelty of being a Malay Muslim woman who wrote and produced music in LA. Plus, it helped that I had a distinctive style of music, primarily a fusion of pop, R&B, and rock, glued together by hooky melody lines and layers of vocals.

Between 1992 and 1997, I wrote and produced songs of several albums' worth of material for most of the major labels, and played a pivotal role in launching the careers of several artists, such as Ziana Zain, KOOL, and Farra.

Unlike in the West, where my Islamic pop CD faced resistance without a distributor because they believe the female voice is *aurat,* another example of a more traditional Muslim society being more accommodating of non-traditional women's roles, I was offered a distribution deal by a Malaysian company!

In a surprising turn of events, a conservative music and publishing house in Malaysia, known as Saba Islamic Media Inc., discovered my music and offered me a three-year distribution deal for its territories, which included Malaysia, Singapore, and Indonesia. To release the album for their audience, the cover of the album was redesigned to reveal only my face and not my hair, creating the illusion of a *hijab,* aligning with their religious beliefs. I was pleasantly surprised that during the promotional tours involving live performances and radio appearances, I was never instructed to wear a *hijab.* The focus was very much on the music and its message, and it was so refreshing for my product to be focused purely on its merits rather than the absurd fixation on the sexuality of a female voice or her hair. The promotional tours included magazine and newspaper interviews, as well as guest speaker at several radio stations in Malaysia and Indonesia. These opportunities stood in stark contrast to the censorship and lack of support I encountered from Muslims in the West.

Fortunately, with the growth and maturity of digital distribution networks, I was able to distribute my music myself. The polished pop production of "Ummah Wake Up" found favor and was quite popular among segments of the American Muslim population. I now encounter young adults who grew up listening to the CD, recounting how their mothers purchased it and had the CD looped on repeat.

Meanwhile, in Malaysia, without having to compromise on quality and artistic freedoms, I won its equivalent of the Grammy, the *Anugerah Industri Musik* for Album of the Year for Siti Nurhalizah in 1999 and in 2004. In 1997, it was exciting to participate in my first music award show put on by TV3, hearing my name called and receiving applause while walking onto the stage, very pregnant, with the popular boy band I produced, KOOL, accompanying me.

As a writer and producer whose work is usually behind the scenes, being upfront, recognized, and applauded in front of a large audience was a very new emotion. It felt good!

Nowadays, with YouTube, it is funny how many decades later my husband is rediscovering my works and appearances online which we share with my adult daughter, who I know experienced the music I was making with her kicking the insides of my belly to the sound of an "808" bass drum. (The 808 was a very popular low-frequency digital sound of a kick drum that vibrated).

My first production work in Malaysia was for BMG, a pop project called "Colors of Love," where I produced an album for an all-girl vocal group from Southeast Asia—Malaysia, Singapore, Indonesia, Philippines, and Thailand, all solo artists in their own right. This project made way for more production work, usually to work on whole albums. In such a scenario, the record companies would rent out an apartment for me. I would rent a car and put in 12–14 hours a day working in the studios. I would spend mornings laying down the music tracks, session musicians would be scheduled to lay down their parts in the afternoon, and vocal recordings in the later afternoon into the evenings. Malaysian singers are notorious for working late, sometimes into the early mornings, whereas I prefer to stop by 10 p.m. at the latest, be in bed by 11 p.m., and get up in the morning to listen to the previous day's work with fresh ears.

Once, I invited my mother to come and visit me at the studio while I was recording vocals with "KOOL". She commented, how "I never realized giving you piano lessons could lead to this!" That was the only time my mother had come to watch me work in my music career.

In Malaysia, I didn't encounter the same level of sexism and stereotypical assumptions from men in the industry as I did in the West. In rooms where I often found myself as the sole woman or behind the mixing board, I never received sexist remarks like, "Oh, you must be the singer." Instead, I enjoyed a considerable degree of creative freedom, being paid to do the work of arrangement, programming, and production of songs. I collaborated closely with predominantly male lyricists and musicians who were both professional and friendly, meaning not having to deal with any sexual tensions.

While I thrived in the realm of songwriting, programming, and production in Malaysia, my experience took a different turn after years of struggling in the United States. I reluctantly conformed to the gendered stereotypes, where the prevailing notion was (and still is) that women primarily wrote lyrics and melody lines, while the roles of composing and producing music tracks fell predominantly within the domain of men. Some men I co-wrote with had no problem with me playing their keyboard and laying down musical arrangements, while a few were rather territorial.

Needless to say, once I switched to writing lyrics and melody lines, my songwriting career took off in the Western world. I was writing with big-name songwriters and producers like Philip Bailey (Earth, Wind, and Fire), Chuckii Booker, and the publishing and production team at Murlyn Music in Sweden, which produced hundreds of world hits, including artists like Britney Spears, and songwriters, and producers in Norway and the UK. Within two years of making such a decision in 2002, my London-based music manager Paul Kennedy secured me a publishing deal with Big Life Music, Ltd., and within five years, thanks to Paul's hard work, I had dozens of songs published worldwide. My songs were translated into different languages including Japanese and Italian, but one of the big hits was a song titled "Hip Hip Hooray" recorded by The Tweenies, a very popular children's television show in the UK, whose live performances sold out stadiums. It makes me smile to know that, as kids, my son-in-law and his younger brother were fans of The Tweenies and even bicycled to one of their concerts.

On many occasions, folks in LA would comment how I was more of an "East Coaster" than "LA." LA folks are notorious for being flaky and always late. I, on the other hand, always kept commitments and was always 5 to 10 minutes early to an appointment or writing sessions. This was the hardwiring by my dad, because for him "being on time is being late."

As a result of the British management team and my natural disposition as being more "East Coast," I preferred collaborating with co-writers and producers in Sweden, Norway, and the UK. They were super-talented, funky, creative, and, most importantly, reliable.

In the street-culture, dog-eat-dog world of the music business, I used to hear the term "Shit floats to the top," meaning that all the awful industry people end up at the top of the food chain. But there were exceptions.

Kevin Moore was a session guitarist whom I used to hire to play guitar parts for my song demos. I paid him $75, a pitiful amount because that was all I could afford. On one occasion, for a session in which I needed his guitar parts, I had to pick him up and drop him off because he didn't have a ride. I know he appreciated that. I felt it. Even though we didn't cross paths very often, we would talk once in a while. And then, out of the blue, he announced that he was putting himself out as a blues artist, got himself a stage name—Keb'Mo'—a manager, and, as the story goes, he became an "overnight" sensation, winning Grammy Awards for best album in the Contemporary Blues category year after year, and for many years.

On a few occasions Keb'Mo' and I would get together to write. Unlike my other writing sessions, we would just talk, old friends having a hearty conversation. It was at one of these get-togethers, when I was feeling let down by a friend, that I allowed myself to be vulnerable because I felt safe to share with Keb' Mo', which resulted in us co-writing the song "One Friend" (Keb'Mo/Moore and Zonneveld, 2014). This song is about a friend who used me to get to my connections that took decades to build. Funny enough, this experience didn't lead the friend to success, while I ended up with an award.

Keb' Mo's writing style, like our conversations, was all heart, as few words as possible, but always on point. In his songwriting style, every word mattered, whereas in the pop style, you would throw in words to fill in a syllable. Overtime, I worked on two albums with Keb' Mo' that resulted in a Grammy nomination in 2011 for "Big Wide Grin", in the children's category, where we lost to Kermit the Frog. In 2014, the album titled "Keep It Simple" garnered a Grammy Award, for which the song "One Friend" was a contributing song, and for that, I received a Grammy certification.

Even with these successes, I can't say that I am fully satisfied. Why? Because I played the industry's game of what a girl can and cannot do. I have a feeling that this circle in my life is incomplete, and I will be returning to close it in the future, and on my terms.

***

Society makes it very hard for a woman to just "be." At every level of society, whether it be in the family unit, in religious communities, corporate, the music business, or even the human rights world, sexism, and patriarchy permeate to hold girls and women back from living their full potential. It is what fuels my indignation, my anger, and my work.

It is from these experiences that I have ingrained in me what "living your full potential" really means. And it is remarkable how hard it is to live to your full potential when we are constantly given a prescribed and confining role.

My mother sometimes scolded me when I laughed too loudly in public, as that was apparently "unbecoming for a girl." This curtailing of my expression is trivial in comparison to what some women and girls experience, especially in some Muslim societies. It is these moments of indignation at these minor infringements of my freedom to express myself that have made me empathize with the grave hardships young women and girls endure in the name of religion and/or culture. It is this empathy that keeps my focus steady on the causes that I work on, and rage that allows me to be unflinching and unapologetic in my defense of their rights.

We know too well how girls are usually deprived of advanced schooling as they are primed for marriage. Priming for marriage in some societies starts as early as nine years old, and in some cultures, this priming includes cutting off the clitoris and stitching up their vaginas, with just enough of a hole for urine, and menstruation to flow. This practice is called Female Genital Mutilation or Cutting (FGM/C). The practice of

FGM goes back for centuries, and its sole purpose is to control women's sexual desire. Some people are trying to sanitize FGM by renaming it as "female circumcision" which is a false equivalence. FGM/C is like cutting off a men's penis. There are thousands more nerves in a woman's clitoris than the tip of a penis, and the practice of cutting has no basis in religion, including Islam. Yet time and time again, religion is often conveniently used to justify FGM, as well as the full slew of rights infringement of women and girls by men and women infused in patriarchal values.

To support my work against the practice of FGM and after a public humiliation from Congresswoman Ilhan Omar on this matter, I was gifted the "Gold Book," by a scholar of Islam, Michael Privot Perso, as an act of solidarity. This book was a compilation of religious edicts from various Muslim scholars and authorities debunking the practice of FGM as "Islamic."

On November 24, 2006, a conference was organized by a German organization, Target, led by a couple, Annette Weber and Rüdiger Nehberg, who were so appalled by the practice that they requested al-Azhar University, a 1,000-year-old Sunni Islam institution, to hold a convening of religious authorities to issue a statement against the practice. The Grand Mufti of Egypt at that time, Ali Gom'a said, "If you pay for the conference, I will make the al-Azhar Conference Center available to you and will offer you my patronage". The outcome of the conference was the publication of the "Gold Book."

A woman's sexuality is also controlled from having to prove her virginity on the first wedding night with a bloody spot on the bed sheet, as if blood is proof of the tearing of the hymen. It is this business of preserving the hymen that millions of girls are not allowed to do sports, thus setting them up to a sedentary and unhealthy lifestyle. So, as you run around doing your sports and gym activities, you're lucky you do not have the burden of worrying about "tearing your hymen diminishing your prospects of marriage."

Fortunately for me, my parents encouraged us to excel in schooling, in careers, to be healthy, to work out, and to compete in sports. It is this backdrop that has given me a positive outlook and context for what a healthy family unit is, and the huge impact that positive encouragement from parents can do for the well-being and mental health of their children. Compared to how I was raised, millions of young girls are not so fortunate. It is appalling how the implementation of the various restrictions of women's and girl's freedom to express themselves, to laugh, to play freely, to experience life, and just to "be" is inflicted on so many levels of society, and in all societies.

It is these injustices that motivate me to do the human rights advocacy that I do. Oftentimes, I don't even know how it is being received or if it even matters. It was therefore a surprise when, in 2016, a student director at the University of Southern California's prestigious Master's film school program emailed me. His name was Omar al-Dakheel, and he wanted to direct a short documentary about me and the work I do, resulting in the film titled *al-imam* (2016) (Photo: al imam with Omar).

**Figure 3:** al imam with Omar

With the approval of his professor, Amanda Pope, who apparently knew about me, Omar and his crew followed me for months, documenting my various activities, including speaking and singing at interfaith events, leading men and women in prayer, and having conversations with my daughter and with an interfaith couple whose wedding I officiated. Sometimes the crew would come to my home early in the morning, with me opening the door still in my pajamas, and other times they would film me warming up my vocals in the car. It also documented the threats I received, the hate messages, and the toll it has taken on the relationship between myself and the conservatives in my family, especially my sister and my mother.

Throughout filming, Omar emphasized the importance of telling my personal stories because "people are not going to care about the organization, but people will feel emotionally attached to the person." This framing and perspective led to a tug-of-war between Omar and me. Eventually, I surrendered to the process, trusting Omar as the storyteller to handle it responsibly, with the condition that I have the final say on the title. With co-producers Sarah Fenton Vance and John Palmer, Omar initially named it "*al-Imam*" with a capital "I," but I insisted on a small "i" to reflect my values of an Islam devoid of hierarchy, where all are equal.

The release of the documentary was a huge film school affair at the Steven Spiegel Theater at University of Southern California; a large poster of the film was on display, with the back of my head, and I was facing a mosque, a symbol of the film's contents, battling patriarchy. The theater was packed with students and their families. I attended with my family and friends, and as I saw myself on screen, I sank into the theater seat. I've always preferred being in the background, which is why I am comfortable as a songwriter and producer, putting the spotlight on the singers I produce. Being so front and center on a huge screen was a very emotionally memorable, cringing experience.

Since then, "*al-imam*" has won the KCET Student's Documentary Award, which qualified it to be screened at the Cannes Film Festival in 2019. It has gone to numerous film festivals, including

Academy-qualifying ones. It made its screening at Kuwait's Sirdab Lab, followed by a discussion on the contents of the documentary by the Kuwaiti Progressive Movement, or *Alharaka Altaqadomia*, and made the pick for digital distribution on Public Broadcasting Service (PBS), National Geographic, and Argo. This short documentary has had a life beyond the usual one festival season, and for eight years, it was still being picked up by festivals and distributors.

Distributions didn't come without its challenges, after all, it is a positive film about a Muslim woman fighting sexism and patriarchy. While it made its debut on National Geographic, the channel's headquarters in Washington, D.C. received a death threat, prompting National Geographic to temporarily take it down. After an emergency meeting of its executive team, and upon further assessment of the threat, the channel decided to put it back online. It is not clear whether the threat came from a radical Muslim or a radical Christian entity. Regardless, I commend the channel for putting it back online.

Having a young Muslim man from the Arab world direct a film about me was a form of acknowledgment of the work I've done through Muslims for Progressive Values (MPV). I knew he would cover the human rights issues I address, particularly those of women, girls, and LGBTQ+ rights, in a manner and with the nuances that a progressive Muslim would inherently understand without me having to explain it. I also knew my story would be framed in a positive light rather than using me to demonize Islam and Muslims. More details on this media experience later.

The injustice most painful to bear is those from our own parents, especially our mothers. Just like my mother's various prohibitions of what I, as a girl, can and cannot do, the implementation of the practice of FGM is often carried out by the womenfolk of the family. But because of my overall positive family upbringing, and as a mother, I can stand in front of many Muslim parents and challenge them to do better for their children.

Fortunately for me, I had an ambitious father who had very high expectations for all his children, including us girls. Never was the idea of marriage planted in my head, instead, my dad pushed me to go to university, to become a doctor, or a professional of some sort. He was the counterbalance to my mother's more sexist mindset. The mantra my father ingrained in me was "make your life count Ani." To understand him is to better understand what I have become.

# 4
# My father and my Malay tradition

My father's accomplishments, strong character, work ethic, and how he instilled these values in my siblings and me, made me curious about his lineage. On different trips back to Malaysia, I would ask relatives and friends about them.

I learned that my paternal grandmother, Bibi binti Rahmat, was a Muslim with roots from Punjab, India, which makes me 25 per cent Punjabi!

My paternal great-grandfather, Tok Nek Samad, (*Tok Nek* in Malay means great grandfather), was a religious teacher and was even considered to be a *waliullah*, or the village religious representative. In Malay culture, the role of a *waliullah*, which translates to "saint" or "holy person," holds immense significance within the community. These individuals are often revered for their deep spiritual knowledge, piety, and commitment to Islam. As the village *waliullah*, Tok Nek Samad's personal dedication to his faith played a pivotal role in guiding and nurturing the spiritual well-being of the community, providing religious education, moral guidance, and strengthening their faith. This elevated status as a *waliullah* underscores Tok Nek Samad's profound influence on the religious and cultural fabric of the Malay community that he served. Unlike today's influencers, who monopolize their social status to benefit financially, Tok Nek Samad was influential and poor.

My paternal grandfather was Awang Osman bin Mohammed Arshad, born June 16, 1870, and died on March 20, 1933, at the age of 63. As it was a Malay culture to give up your child for adoption into a family that could provide for the child's well-being, Tok Nek Samad gave him up for adoption to the State of Kedah's Royal Family, and grew up in the Royal Palace. Like his father, he grew up to be a Qur'an teacher and taught the children of the Royal family. After marrying his wife Bibi, they were transferred to Penang, where he taught at the Penang Free School, an English medium school, and where he continued to care for the royal children, the likes of Tuanku Abdul Rahman, who eventually became the first Prime Minister of Malaysia.

It made me pause to learn about this history of spiritual teachers and leaders on my father's side, and it made me wonder how I never learned about this history before and what would my father think of my work now, utilizing religion in affirming human rights, and my nurturing for the spiritual well-being of Progressive Muslims.

On June 4, 1925, my father, Abdul Khalid bin Awang Osman, was born in Penang, Malaysia, the fifth of nine children. All the children attended the Penang Free School, and as a result of their English education, they were afforded many more career opportunities, for which they excelled. When I think about how numerous and successful my paternal lineage is, I feel tremendous pride about my own ancestry, and I wish I could have a conversation with them.

It is important to note, in the British colonization of Malaysia, the opportunities my father's family had by way of their British schooling didn't come with preconditions, whereas many other colonies in Africa didn't fare as well. The remanence of the Belgium colonization of Burundi, a Grand Mufti of Burundi I had befriended shared how at one time in history, if you wanted to get ANY education you had to attend a Catholic school, and to do that, you had to change your name to a Christian one. He changed his name to Philip.

Let that sink in.

For me growing up, my last name was always Osman, as we were being identified by our grandfather's last name, which is the Western way of naming, while my Malaysian identity card reads Zuriani binti Abdul Khalid—Zuriani daughter of Abdul Khalid. This is because the "binti" in between the first and last names is a reference to a person's lineage, that's why my father's name was Abdul Khalid bin (son of) Awang Osman. Malaysian Muslims inherited this method of naming from the Arab traders who introduced Islam to the Malay Peninsular coastal towns in 674 CE.

My married name is Zuriani Zonneveld, but because we usually shorten our names to one or two syllables, my nickname is Ani.

My family's history is a tale of resilience and ambition, woven through generations. It begins with the loss of my paternal grandparents when my father was just eight years old. It is in our culture for the eldest male and female sibling to shoulder the responsibility, sacrificing their own educational journeys. My oldest uncle, whose name echoes through our family lore, becomes the sole breadwinner. Meanwhile, my aunt embraced the role of a surrogate mother, ensuring the younger ones were nurtured and cared for.

Despite these challenges, the flame of determination burned within the family, not much different than the fire in my belly. Every sibling, against all odds, not only completed their school education, but many completed higher learning. The spirit of overachievement and a profound work ethic propelled them toward success in their chosen paths, and this motivation had an added sense of urgency, given Malaysia's newfound independence from the British in 1957.

In this constellation of achievers, a name that resonates with both familial pride and historical significance is my uncle Dato Sir Mohamed Sheriff bin Awang Osman. His ascent to become the Governor of the State of Kedah in 1948 was no small feat. Such roles were typically reserved for those of aristocratic lineage, but he shattered these barriers, becoming the first commoner to hold such a position. In a society that is led by monarchy, just like the British societal structure where titles like Prince, Sir, and Lord marked your class in society, Tunku, Syed, and Wan denoted royalty or of an esteemed heritage. My uncle's achievement, a layman, was a resounding testament to merit and was awarded with the titles "Dato" and "Sir."

Another uncle, Professor Dr Mustapha bin Awang Osman, was renowned as the first Malay surgeon. He graduated in medicine from the University of Hong Kong in 1924. He made history as the first Malay surgeon appointed as Surgeon General by both the Japanese Military Administration during the Second World War occupation of Malaya and, later, by the British during their rule. The British colonizers usually appointed a fellow Brit to this high post, and my uncle was the first Asian to be appointed to such a high post.

In the broader context of Malaysia's history, a pivotal moment emerged as the British Empire relinquished its hold, ushering Malaysia's independence after 250 years of colonization. This period was rife with challenges and opportunities, offering a fertile ground for patriots like my family members. My uncle, Muhammad Sheriff, stood as a representative of 13 Malay rulers at the United Nations, embodying the spirit of a true *Perjuang,* or warrior. It is for this reason that I have titled my memoir, "The Unlikely Social Justice Warrior."

My father, Abdul Khalid Awang Osman, was a young politician during this transformative era. He was a member of the Parti Perikatan, the Malay political party founded to play a pivotal role in negotiating the terms for independence from the British. His dedication to the cause led him to becoming a member of the United Malay National Organization (UMNO). In the first election of a newly independent country, he ran as a representative in Kuala Kerai in the state of Kelantan and emerged victorious. Kelantan is a very conservative state that can be compared to Alabama, and my father winning a seat there is like having

Kamala Harris representing the state of Alabama in the House. To this day, my dad is the only UMNO member to have won an election in Kelantan.

From a parliamentarian, he rose to become the Assistant Minister of Rural Development, then to become the Deputy Minister of Commerce and Industry, and then Deputy Minister of Interior. He was then appointed as an ambassador to Indonesia, The Netherlands, Germany, Sudan, Lebanon, Egypt, Nepal, and India.

Growing up as a national of a newly independent country meant there was a nation to build. Having a father whose life was defined by making this new country flourish meant he was driven by relentless work, perpetual learning, and a pursuit of self-improvement. Every moment was precious to him, and he guarded his time zealously. I, too, inherited this trait, often declaring, "Waste your time all you want, but don't you dare waste mine."

My father and I had a complex relationship. As a daughter, I was tasked with the cultural ritual of greeting him every morning in his home office with a kiss on his hand, a practice repeated in the evening before bedtime. Our conversations, especially during my younger years, were limited and sparse. I admit I was afraid of him, a stern figure with a no-nonsense persona. However, come Sundays, he transformed into an entirely different human being.

In the houses I grew up in, the family living room held a special place. It was perched on the second floor, informal and comfortable, devoid of servants or caregivers. This space was our private sanctuary, where I would present my report cards, outline a meticulously planned timetable for my waking hours, and face his reproach if I strayed from my own schedule.

Sundays in this room were our musical sanctuary, a day where I was allowed to get off the treadmill of piano practice, schoolwork, and tight time-tables, and it was here that my father let his guard down, turning into a DJ wearing just a white singlet and a *sarong*. His musical tastes were diverse, a playlist that included traditional Malay folk tunes, patriotic songs blended in with the timeless melodies of Nat King Cole, the soulful tunes of Louise Armstrong, opera, and the latest pop hits that echoed the contemporary beat of our times, like Heintje, The Osmonds, The Beatles, and Nancy Sinatra. Many decades later, I still know the melody and lyrics to all these songs.

With his collection of favorite music on a reel-to-reel tape player blasting, he would sing along, his baritone voice revealing a stern father softened, a wide smile, and an even happier smiling eyes. I could see he was happy, almost childlike even, and that made me smile inside. The simple joy music brings reminds me that even the most formidable personalities find solace in music. It is the way music disarms people, and the science behind emotional memory has also informed how I utilize music in the human-rights work I do.

I called my dad *bapak,* which means father in Malay. Music had this magical effect on him, as it did on me. While *bapak* pretended he was singing on stage, I became an ardent observer, studying the intricate musical arrangements, the placement of melody structures and how a word is married to a note. It was in those stolen glances and my attention to the notes that my own understanding of music took root, nurtured by the melodies and the different genres that echoed through our home. You could say, my dad was the first to expose me to music, which shaped the way I write and produce songs.

His love for music was apparent, and so was his fervor for Malaysia's independence and his governmental duties. To advance the spirit of patriotism, he even ventured into song-writing, crafting a few patriotic compositions that some deemed "too nationalistic." The tale of these songs remains a mystery, a hidden chapter in his legacy. I stumbled upon this revelation recently, which even my mother does not know what became of them. It was yet another chord in the symphony of my father's life, purposeful, innovative in his problem-solving, and discovering how similar I am to him.

*****

My childhood was adorned with the presence of hired car-egivers, two young Malay women who happened to be from my mother's side of the family. Their responsibilities stretched far beyond just looking after my younger brother and me. They were our caretakers, our bathers, our dressers, and our feeders. In the tapestry of our home, they were the unsung heroes, tending to not just us, but also managing the family's laundry, ironing, and the meticulous task of keeping our home spotless.

Their tenure with us, however, was transient. Whenever my father, in his diplomatic role, was posted to another country, these young women would bid us farewell, making way for new faces to fill their roles. A pattern emerged—that they would return home after approximately four years, stepping into the next chapter of their lives, often marked by marriage. Alongside their presence, my uncle Mak Bakar, a constant in our lives, ensured we always had a trio of helpers accompanying us on our journeys, shaping our household dynamics for a significant 16 year stretch.

When I was about seven years old in Egypt, we had one new addition to our household. My parents hired an Egyptian, Suad, to help around the house, and before long, my mother and Suad became very close. Suad taught us about "halawa," an old waxing tradition dating back to Cleopatra. Once a month, my mother and I would be treated to waxing sessions, reappearing with smooth, hairless legs, underarms, and arms. When we left Egypt for India, Suad came along with us, and when we returned to Malaysia, she moved there with us as well. After some years, though, Suad left to return to Egypt to care for her father, and sadly, we lost touch with her.

Despite the presence of these helpers, the ethos of our household was firmly grounded in the values of responsibility and respect. The expansive official ambassador's residences were such that we often found ourselves in our own little worlds within its vast confines. Communication was facilitated through an intercom system in selected rooms, like my father's home office, living and dining room, kitchen, and hallways that allowed us to connect with each other at the push of a button and without having to call out loud. Yet, this convenient form of communication was largely untouched by us children.

Meanwhile, as a child, we were taught to dutifully follow the rule: if you desired something, you approached the helpers in person. It was a practice instilled in us, a subtle yet important lesson in humility and respect. It was an upbringing unlike the many abusive manners, and frankly, criminal, in which many in the Gulf States treat their housekeepers from poorer countries such as Indonesia, Somalia, Bangladesh, India, and others.

My upbringing was emblematic of how we were raised— respect for all people, and till this day, I judge those around me by how they treat the poor, the down-and-trodden, and the discriminated.

Although having helpers waiting on you, and a driver on your beck on call, is comfortable living, as a mom, I wanted to raise my child myself, assuming the many roles that come from doing so. On a few occasions, my daughter laments how lucky I was to have a driver. Yes, driving in traffic in LA to and from school takes up a lot of time, but I am much more engaged in my daughter's schooling, sports, arts activities, and birthday parties than my mother ever was.

From the age of five, my parents scheduled me for private piano lessons, which I continued to take until I was 17. At the Malaysian Ambassador's residence where we lived in Bonn, Cairo, and New Delhi, we were privileged to have pianos furnished. In Germany, it was a Steinway grand piano, while in Egypt and India, they were upright Yamaha pianos. In India, we had a dedicated "music room" where my parents bought us an organ, *a sitar, a tabla,* and an acoustic guitar—instruments that I picked up and for which I had formal lessons. We also had a drum set for my younger brother, which sat almost untouched most of the time.

I don't remember the name of my music teacher in India, but he was an elderly Christian man. I know that he was Christian because I attended his organ recital at his church. With his recommendation, my mother had me compete in piano recitals in which I came third on one occasion. I also sat for the annual piano examinations by the Royal Schools of Music.

Throughout the 16 years as an ambassador's daughter, I remember my dad organizing extravagant cultural activities, creating community and friendships. He was a sociable person, and it was reflected in his activities. One particularly big production was an annual cultural event. Not only would he get the embassy staff involved, but he would also rope in the many Malaysian students studying abroad, and of course, me. My older siblings didn't live with us, and my younger brother was either too young or not interested in participating in the activities.

The cultural events would be a reproduction of a Malay wedding, and several traditional dance numbers and the Malay *silat,* a martial art, would be performed as part of an entertainment program for the acting bride and groom. To end the program, with the couple seated-in-state, or *bersanding,* VIP guests such as government representatives and diplomats would be invited up to the stage to sprinkle *bunga air* (scented water with flowers), raw yellow rice, and flower petals for fertility. As a gift, guests would be handed out *bunga telur,* boiled eggs that are attached to an elaborate paper flower. Over the years my role evolved from playing usher to the VIPs, decked out in traditional attire, to helping with the logistics of organizing.

In the *silat*, the *kris*—a double-edged, wavy dagger, a weapon and a spiritual object played a prominent role. It is used by trained martial warriors of *silat,* and to become one, you have to be spiritually sound. In the Malay tradition, predominantly found in Malaysia and Indonesia, the *kris* protects its owner and is known to have magical powers.

As a dedication to my work, my brother Azahari drew a painting for me and about me called "The Warrior" an image of a woman with a *kris* strapped to her back.

At the age of eight, my father taught me how to play table tennis. We had a scheduled one-and-a-half hours of practice every weekday afternoon before dinner. For a while, I would lose to him. As time progressed, each week I was losing by smaller margins, until one day, I finally beat him. I was elated, maybe too elated, because I found myself looking at his downcast smile, a sad smile, probably thinking, "She doesn't need this old man anymore." Until today, I occasionally still play table tennis, a game where my son-in-law and I get really competitive. And still today, if I come across a table, I'll be playing, like a kid.

My father loved to dance. At my sister's wedding in Malaysia, she and her husband didn't dance as they are very conservative, so he danced with me to the traditional Malay *joget.* On one occasion, he invited a traditional Malay music ensemble to play at our residence in Bonn, Germany. I was about five years old, in my pajamas, and upon hearing the "live" music downstairs, I put on my housecoat, intent on joining the fun. Lo and behold, the living room furniture was cleared off to the walls, the musicians on one side of the room, the carpets rolled up and put away, revealing the wood floor, and there were my parents dancing away! My mother tried to shoo me away, but my father smiled and the other adults cheered at seeing me dance.

From a young age, I learned traditional Malay dances from my uncle Mak Bakar, so once I was back in Malaysia in 1978, at the age of 16, I spent my time exploring Kuala Lumpur's cultural and music scene, and it was rich!

I spent a lot of my time immersing myself in traditional cultural practices, bettering my dance skills with lessons provided for free at the Ministry of Culture, and learning to play the *gamelan*, an ensemble of various brass instruments that you play with a mallet. I got really good at the dancing that I auditioned for and was accepted as a member of the Kuala Lumpur Federal Territory dance troupe. This is equivalent to being a member of a dance troupe that represents your city. As a dancer, I got to be a regular teenage girl, just like the others. Nobody knew who my dad was, I traveled to and from rehearsals by bus, a far cry from being chauffeured around in a limo. Unlike the days when my attire was restricted and where I always looked "presentable," now, I wore jeans, T-shirts, and flip-flops, I was sweaty, unkept, and happy.

Whereas my outings were incredibly restricted as an ambassador's daughter, in Malaysia I was cut loose. I would check out the live bands at clubs, returning late into the night on the last bus. I befriended the musicians and eventually played keyboards in "AsiaBeat", a jazz fusion band founded by drummer and percussionist Lewis Pragasam. The band was offered a record deal with Columbia Broadcasting System (CBS), and I was excited to be part of that.

It was in this independent spirit that I began to assert myself a little more than I would have dared, announcing the record deal offer. And it was then that my father and I had our first screaming match. It ended with my father commanding, "You are not doing music! You are going to college in the United States, and you are going to do something useful with your life!"

Looking back, I cannot say I had a very close relationship with my father as a child. I walked on eggshells most of the time whenever he was around, and I didn't feel confident enough to speak my mind. The hardest part of our relationship was when I was 17 years old. But I guess that could be said for most 17 year olds.

My father was a strict disciplinarian. He had a reputation of being a hard worker, driven to make something useful out of his life. I learned this while visiting my friend, the Argentine ambassador's daughter. Upon learning I was the Malaysian Ambassador's daughter, the Argentine Ambassador admiringly told me, "Your father is such a hardworking man!" I could see for myself how, upon returning from the office, he was mostly in his study room, always consumed with reading and learning. But it made me proud to hear it from a stranger.

He was not one to settle for the status quo, nor was he the kind to brag. He was always striving to do things better, differently, challenging himself and those around him. I learned about this on television when I happened to watch *"Hari Ini Dalam Sejarah"*, which translates to "Today in History", where, in 1968, my father signed a Technical Cooperation Agreement with the West German government to bring their engineering expertise to Malaysia. Newly independent, Malaysia was an underdeveloped country, and we needed all the transfer of technology we could get if we were to advance. For this work, in 1967, he received the Iron Cross Second Class from the President of the Federal Republic of Germany, Heinrich Lübke, and again in 1970 from President Gustav Walter Heinemann. This award is now framed and sits in my living room, a constant reminder of his mantra: "make your life count."

This was not the only award he received. He received similar awards from President Sadat of Egypt, and one from President Morarji Desai of India.

The bar was set really high for us, for his sons as well as his daughters. He kept a folder for each one of us with all our records, and his ideas on what we should do with our lives, never mind if we were cut out for it or even slightly interested in it. For him, it was imperative that each one of us contributed to the development of Malaysia, and to make our lives count.

While I was at university in the United States, my father and I exchanged letters, and reading them back, I could see that our relationship was changing from that of an authoritative parent to treating me like an adult. Maybe it was his age or his ailing heart that made him more reconciliatory; regardless, it felt good to finally be respected as an adult. Even though showing affection was not something my parents were very good at, my dad always signed off with "yours lovingly."

In 1985, I graduated from Northern Illinois University with a double major in Political Science and Economics. My parents attended my graduation, probably finding it hard to believe that I graduated! I think my dad was particularly proud that I gave the commencement speech at the Political Science Department's graduation ceremony.

It was at that point that I announced that I was moving to Los Angeles to pursue music rather than return back to Malaysia to join the Foreign Service.

By this time, we had a much healthier relationship. In the last few years of his life, he shared his feelings with me about my siblings, my mother, the challenges in his business venture, and his thoughts about going into public service, again. I would call him periodically back in the days when international phone calls were extremely expensive, somewhere around $1.35 per minute. One day, on February 12, we had an exceptionally long and warm conversation. We talked about his life in retirement, caught up with family matters, and, of course, politics. My heart was full. When we were about to hang up, I was close to saying "I love you, *bapak*," but I didn't.

Twenty-four hours later, my older brother Rahman called to tell me my family had just buried my dad. The date was February

14, 1986. Islamic burial traditions edict that the deceased is washed, wrapped in white cloth, prayed for, and buried within 24 hours, which is what my family did.

My father had a weak heart and had suffered several heart attacks over the last few decades of his life. After speaking to me, he took his heart medication but choked on it. That assertion of choking was enough to result in a heart attack that, this time, took his life. My mother was on the floor, cradling him on her lap when he died. Even though, I was thousands of miles away, I was the last person he spoke to.

My dad's passing was announced in Malaysian newspapers, and the Sultan of Kedah and other dignitaries paid their last respects at my parents' home.

I wish my dad were around for me now. I could use a mentor, the wisdom of his years in creating opportunities for rural folks, his pragmatic approach in diplomacy and politics to advance the economic and development opportunities of a young country.

# 5
# Not Muslim enough and too Muslim

I have come a long way from the days of rediscovering my identity. Am I Muslim? If so, why? Today, I firmly identify myself as a progressive Muslim and a human rights advocate, which brings me to another level of challenges. Identifying myself as a progressive Muslim and a human rights defender in one sentence is tricky—and here's why...

When I am challenging the Muslim patriarchal individuals and institutions for their misogynistic, homophobic, and supremacist interpretations of Islam, I am often told I am not Muslim enough because I do not wear a *hijab* (the headscarf), that I don't read Arabic, and that I am not traditionally trained. My rebuttal to their attempts at discrediting me is simple—I use passages of the Quran that make no claim that a Muslim woman needs to cover her hair; that Arabic is not the only language of God, and that every person has the responsibility to use their God-given brain to think critically and to rationalize.

Believe it or not, this is actually the easier challenge. The harder challenge is being recognized as legitimate by secular and ex-Muslims, as well as secular non-Muslims on the Left and the Right. In other words, just about everyone else.

With the backdrop of 9/11, it was evident Muslims were being represented by conservatives. This would be equivalent to the Orthodox Jews representing all American Jews. If that happened, Reform Jews would throw a fit, given their overwhelming majority. Similarly, progressive Muslims are the majority, but they are barely visible.

Muslims for Progressive Values (MPV) was therefore founded out of this need for representation, and for the majority of American Muslims who for various reasons have left the mosque and needed community. In the summer of 2007, along with other like minded Muslims, I and others organized the founding conference at Sarah Lawrence College, in New York. Those who played an important role in the founding of MPV included Kareem Elbayar, Pamela Taylor, Imam Daayiee Abdullah, el-Farouk Khaki, Mike Ghouse, Jack Fertig, and Sabahat Ashraf. Along with others, we spent two days finalizing the mission and vision, and the founding members voted me President, tasked with registering the organization as a non-profit and running the day to day business.

In the early days of founding MPV, asserting our identity as "progressive" within the Muslim community was met with resistance, often leading to heated conversations. Mainstream Muslims would react indignantly, exclaiming, "So I'm not progressive?!" Their defensive tone was palpable.

I would calmly counter, asking a simple question: "Do you support a woman's full agency and equality, including the right to lead both men and women in prayer? And do you stand for LGBTQ+ rights?" Invariably, their response would be a resounding "no." To this, I would assert, "Then, by definition, you are not progressive."

Many years later, my long-time friend Rabbi Jim Kaufman observed, "Ani, you should have called the organization Muslims for Traditional Values, as you are reclaiming what is rightly Islam". That may be true, but by labeling ourselves "progressive" we are able to assert our own identity and recreate traditions that truly reflect the Quran's egalitarian values, much like the way Reform and Reconstructionist Judaism have done.

Defining our values and anchoring our identity in them was no easy feat. We meticulously crafted our principles, ensuring that they were deeply rooted in Islamic theology and traditions, both ancient and contemporary, stripped of misogynistic cultures and patriarchal structures. It is this foundation that gives us relevance and has propelled the progressive Muslim movement beyond the borders of the US.

For secular and ex-Muslims, the task of disentangling their cultural upbringing—infused with Islam—from the pure teachings of the Quran is a daunting challenge. I empathize with the trauma caused by decades of emotional and mental abuse in the name of religion, leading to a deep-seated hatred for Islam. During my travels, I encountered resistance firsthand. In Tunisia, after introducing our #ImamsForShe initiative, I faced vehement criticism from secular Tunisian feminists, with comments such as, "how dare you put Islam and human rights in the same sentence!" In another instance, a young, educated Tunisian man confessed his atheism. When I shared a Quranic verse affirming the right to choose one's religion or no religion, he remained skeptical. So I asked him to look up the Quranic verse: 2:256. He read the Quran off his phone "There is no compulsion in faith", and he stared at me in utter disbelief. I left him with a simple truth:

"You've been lied to."

The struggle to bridge these gaps in understanding persists, and our commitment to progressive values remains unwavering. Over the years, we've partnered with several scholars of Islam to produce educational content made accessible to the public, content that is usually exclusive to the world of academia. To reach a broader population, we have also translated our content into Urdu and Arabic.

After more than 17 years of advocating for human rights, the good news is that now organizations and universities have recognize the viability of tackling human rights violations from the context of Islam, and what better way than to have a practitioner teach a class sharing in the lived realities rather than just a theory. In the last seven years I have been asked to teach classes at UCLA, Yale, private highschools, the Institute of Social Ethics (ISE), the University of Lucerne in Switzerland, and many more.

In 2015, I found myself at an ex-Muslim conference in London. Conservative and traditional Muslims consider ex-Muslims as apostates. Over the years, I have vehemently advocated against the prosecution of ex-Muslims. They are often vilified by conservative Muslims, and in many Muslim-majority countries, depending on their version of the sharia law, apostates face jail time, death threats, or death sentences. On a panel at this conference, I defended the rights of ex-Muslims. Armed with verses from the Quran, quotes from Muslim philosophers, and the latest position from Morocco's highest religious authorities stating, "Apostasy and blasphemy have no basis in Islam but are political tools," I thought my argument was unassailable. Little did I expect the backlash I received. Instead of welcoming a narrative that affirmed their rights within a theological framing, I was met with accusations of "lying" and was drowned in hate. Also at the receiving end of this hate was another panelist, Karima Bennoune, who was the United Nations Special Rapporteur for cultural rights at the time.

Activists who are exclusive and intolerant in their positioning don't do their cause a service. Instead of embracing allies who happen to identify as Muslims to help bring along others, they prefer to remain a victim, and spew hate. Sitting in the audience during my presentation was Richard Dawkins, the well-known anti-theist atheist. I wonder what he thought of the drama. From what I can tell of his posts on X, he either didn't learn anything from my presentation, or it is easier to continue his brand of perpetuating hate of Islam than acknowledging an enlightened version. This for me is just another example of tribalism, othering a group to make yourself look better. It is also intellectually dishonest.

Yes, I was accused of deception for simply speaking the truth. I get it, the wounds from religious trauma cut deep, but it seems easier for some to cling to anti-Islam sentiments than to challenge the very foundation of their hatred, which has become intertwined with their identities. On Reddit, ex-Muslims produce an abundance of scorn and misinformation about Muslims and Islam, reinforcing the very patriarchal and radical theology progressive Muslims debunk as "truth." I don't understand what they have to gain from creating enemies and hate for regular Muslims. I know for a fact, being an ex-Muslim opens up a lot of opportunities and funding in ways we progressives could only dream of. The book deals, with speaking opportunities, the extensive secular platforms both in-person and virtual, are not accessible to progressive Muslims. A narrative of Islam that imbues inclusivity and human rights negates the violent image of Muslims and Islam, and especially that of Muslim men.

The demonization of Muslim men is quite easy when they have perpetrated violence against humanity, women, and girls in the name of their version of Islam. This has resulted in the normalization of anti-Islam and anti-Muslim sentiment by the mainstream media and politicians, especially in Europe, and particularly since Israel's war on Gaza. So much so that in July 2024, when a group of young Taylor Swift fans were stabbed resulting in three deaths, the false claim that the crime was committed by a Muslim immigrant caught fire as truth. As a result, several asylum shelters, mosques, and Muslim-owned businesses in the UK were attacked and a few burned as revenge.

The fact that such a lie was believable on such a massive scale is because of the constant negative personification of Muslims, especially of Muslim men. If Europeans, especially their governments are so serious about countering radicalism, why do they not support progressive Muslims? After all, we defy extremism at the risk of our own lives, we establish progressive communities that promote egalitarian values, which happen to coincide with democratic values. Women imams in the US and Europe should be at the table with policymakers, but instead, it is still the patriarchs who dominate the space at the exclusion of diverse Muslim perspectives. But, if you're an ultra-Zionist Muslim, you are set!

In our inclusive communities, women and men lead prayer. Our form of prayers is the same as traditional ones, except we make sure to instruct the congregation that we don't segregate, that families can pray together, and that trans folks can stand where they are most comfortable. We brand this "Mecca-style" because we don't segregate in Mecca. If one is not comfortable with an unsegregated manner, men can stand on one side, women on the other. This way, everyone can find a comfortable space for themselves. It is a physical expression of egalitarianism.

My question to the European governments: Are we women imams not at the table because the existence of women imams undermines the average Westerner's belief that Islam is misogynistic, homophobic, and barbaric?

In an effort to bulldoze through that Western patriarchal glass ceiling, in February 2024, Muslim men, Brahim Laytouss, and Michael Privot, organized the first Lady Imam Conference in Brussels convening women imams from Europe and the Unites States. The result was the establishment of a Women Imam Network, with the goal of becoming a nonprofit in the European Union. I purposefully mention the support of these Muslim men as my way of shattering the unfair, perceived reputation they have.

Right-Wing Christians justify their hatred of Islam and Muslims by utilizing the same *hadith* and distorted versions of Islam regurgitated by both radical Muslims and ex-Muslims. This version, the same one that has inflicted so much pain on women, homosexuals, secular, and ex-Muslims, is unfortunately the lens through which many view Islam. Having appeared on several right-wing television programs, I've noticed a common theme: they love to scorn how Muslim men treat Muslim women, the violence perpetuated in the name of Islam, and sharia law, which is all amusing to me, as they share the exact same values!

As an example, laws legislated by the Christian Right, such as anti-abortion laws or the criminalization of trans people, to name a few, are based on their understanding of the Bible, whereas Muslims legislate sharia law based on their understanding of the Quran. Both are man-made sets of laws as extrapolated by their respective understanding of their religious text. What the Christian Right is legislating is nothing short of Christian "sharia law."

Hate and intolerance of "the other" has a remarkable ability to override rationality, except on one memorable occasion.

In 2013, I was invited to speak and sing at the Wild Goose Festival in North Carolina, a progressive Christian festival of music, books, art, theater, and "courageous conversations." I shared the stage with prominent progressive Christian theologians, including Brian McLaren. My presentations are usually interspersed with original compositions of spiritual songs, and the title of my talk on that occasion was "What is Progressive Islam." After a presentation, I usually mingle around and talk to attendees. An elderly man waved me to the edge of the stage, and I obliged.

"Hi," he said

"Hello," I responded with a smile. He paused before blurting out, "I hate all Muslims and everything about Islam," and then he started to cry quietly. I touched his shoulder. He continued, "But after listening to you speak and sing….my hate is gone."

I was very moved by his honesty, and he taught me a lesson to always give people the benefit of the doubt, that is, haters don't necessarily want to hate.

While the agenda of the Christian Right and ex-Muslims is very clear, secular, and religious non-Muslims on the Left are a confusing lot. As progressives, many have also accepted patriarchal Islam as legitimate and do not accept progressive Muslims as "real Muslims." In the early years of establishing MPV, without fail, I would be asked, "How come you're not wearing a *hijab*?"

After my presentation at a program titled "You can be a Muslim in many ways" at Kvinko in 2012 in Denmark, during the question-and-answer session, a man in the audience asked me, "You are a very rational person, so why are you still a Muslim?" My response was and still is, "I am rational because I am a progressive Muslim."

In the intricate dance of politics and faith, I've found myself standing at the crossroads, a progressive Muslim woman challenging the norms, not just within Islam, but also in the broader context of human rights and social justice. It's a journey that's taken me from the hallowed halls of the United Nations to heated debates within the American political landscape. After speaking at a United Nations conference Commission on the Status of Women in 2004, an elderly Jewish woman came up to me and said, "Your presentation and argument for women's rights is interesting, but why do you have to bring up Islam?"

As a feminist, aren't we supposed to recognize everyone and uplift everyone's rights? Frankly, if the secular human rights narrative is so effective in addressing injustice, then why are human rights abuses, especially those in the name of religion, still rampant? The answer is because it doesn't work. Hardcore secularists can sometimes be just as intolerant as the religious Right in their insistence that only *their* language, *their* values, *their* way is right.

The clash between religious beliefs and universal human rights often feels like an uphill battle. Secular institutions, like the United Nations and the European Union, although well-intentioned, sometimes miss the nuances of Islamic human rights framing, treating the concept as an oxymoron. Their apprehension of this framework is the result of a fear of religion.

One secular community that is clear-eyed and open-hearted toward a faith organization such as MPV is Sholem. It's a Jewish community anchored in social justice, critical of Israel's occupation of Palestine, and one that celebrates its cultures without God. For the past 17 years, I have joined them for their Yom Kippur service as a lead guest singer with their choir for the song "Peace, Salaam, Shalom." The song was composed by Pat Humphries and Sandy Opatow in 2001 following the events of September 11.

In America, the progressive Left is very in tune to protecting minority rights, including Muslims, but turn a blind eye to the internal human rights abuses within the Muslim community, even while they would never tolerate similar human rights violations within their own orthodox co-religionists.

Child and forced marriages are an issue in the US just as FGM is. A lesbian child is much more likely to be forced into a marriage to a straight man to "cure" homosexuality. This is definitely the case in states where marriage age is 16 with parental consent. The term "parental consent" means the parents have signed off on the marriage, regardless whether the child is a willing participant or not. This is problematic when most of the underage girls are not married off to a fellow 16-year-old, but to an adult man. In 2024, child marriage is still legal in 37 states.

Like child and forced marriages, FGM still persists within the United States. FGM is deemed torture by the United Nations and is described as a violent act with physical and mental trauma. In 2005, the US had an anti-FGM legislation in place, and in 2019, two doctors in Detroit were charged by the federal government for practicing FGM secretly after office hours at their private clinic. Girls as young as seven years old were transported from Michigan and Minnesota for this torturous ritual. In 2019, the federal judge threw the case out on a technicality, deemed that the federal law was overreaching, resulting in the US not having an anti-FGM law in place.

As a partner of the "U.S. End FGM/C Network," a coalition to eradicate FGM, we used to meet regularly to strategize for the amendment and passage of a new anti-FGM law. Backing the network is the Wallace Global Fund. Unless you are a deep-pocketed lobbyist, good luck getting attention on this issue, not to mention the swift passage of a bill through Congress. This was made more challenging when we didn't have the support of the public, who were largely oblivious to the fact that FGM was being practiced in the US. This blind spot was a huge hurdle to getting a new law passed.

American policymakers and the media are wonderful at pointing out the ills of other cultures, the human rights abuses in other countries, and how they should change. And yes, we should champion against child and forced marriages and against FGM globally, but we should also clean up our own backyard, as these practices are still rife in the US, and we can only do that when there is a healthy public debate around these issues. This should have been covered by the media, whose job it is to inform the general public.

In 2019, a "Muslim Caucus" conference was organized in D.C. It was a convening for the American-Muslim community to discuss issues that should be debated and to set priorities for selecting a candidate to vote for.

I vividly recall my encounter with Congresswoman Ilhan Omar of Minnesota. As she has millions of followers, I wanted her to become an advocate on the issue of FGM by tweeting once a month to educate the general public and by raising the fact that, in 2020, we did not have an anti-FGM law in place. Given the fact that as a coalition we were unable to secure a meeting with her on this matter, I thought this would be an opportunity for the cause. Upon raising this issue with her in this public forum, she unfortunately took it personally, that is, I raised the issue of FGM *because* she was a Muslim. I was quickly silenced and publicly berated by her with a humiliating slapdown. This issue should have been very relevant to her, especially since two of the children cut were from her own Congressional district in Minnesota.

The incident, while humiliating, also revealed a stark truth: the fight for justice often comes at a personal cost. The room erupted into cheers for her disrespectful slapdown, and the media coverage on these few seconds was overwhelming. It went viral to all corners of the world, and I am not exaggerating. Helping me craft a public response to this exchange were Maryum Saifee, a steering committee member of the US End FGM/C Network and Kevin Jennings who was co-chair of MPV's Board of Trustees. In the following six-week span after that "exchange," my name, Ilhan's, and FGM were mentioned 320 million times in the media. This data was provided to me by a firm in the public relations business with a platform to track and target media outlets, a service they were trying to sell to me as the representative of MPV.

This enormous number of media mentions highlighted how powerful negative headings and stories can be. Like they say, "there's no such thing as negative publicity."

In the midst of this chaos, sensationalized headlines, and misplaced outrage, it became a teaching tool, and that is, how easily crucial topics could be overshadowed by media spins and political agendas.

I discovered who my true allies were, I learned the power of media framing, and faced a harshness at a level that was cruel, simply for advocating against torture of children in front of a supposedly progressive crowd. Even EU executives sitting in Brussels and Geneva, whom I've partnered with for their commitment to the UN Declaration of Human Rights, questioned me and privately criticized me. I was also accused of being "Islamophobic" simply for raising the issue to a fellow Muslim. And by the way, this "Islamophobic" accusation is being abused much in the way as any criticism of Israeli policies are "anti-Semitic." It does tremendous disservice to the real cases of Islamophobia and anti-Semitism. Although we now finally have a comprehensive Federal anti-FGM law, signed into law by President Trump, I might add, we still have ways in discouraging this illegal practice, both within and outside of our borders.

The incident also underscored the importance of reminding myself to stay laser-focused on the causes that matter most. The noise was overbearing, and it was a herculean effort to turn myself inward for some peace. What I find is that when you are in the "game" enough, there will be many distractions and detractors. When the spotlight is on you, it is easy to slip into ego, self-indulgence, and the trappings of arrogance. What keeps me rooted in my mission and vision has always been to keep asking myself, "Why am I doing this? Who is to gain from it?" I measure the words I say, and I hold myself accountable against these questions in every word I utter and in everything I write and do.

In the intricate web of media and societal expectations, I found myself trapped in predefined roles, much like the molds that women are pressured to fit into. In the music business, women are pigeonholed into writing melody lines, and as a Muslim woman, we are supposedly oppressed. The world had its preconceived notions about what my identity should signify and the limits of my voice, even in a supposedly "free," democratic society.

The media's portrayal of Muslims often adheres to rigid stereotypes, perpetuating misconceptions about Islam. I've been mistaken for a non-Muslim due to my last name, occasionally a Jew, and have ended up in email chains in which Islam and Muslims are discussed derogatorily.

As a progressive Muslim in America, what I stand for undermines the "Poor Muslim woman" narrative that is favored by the media. However, the media, particularly on the Left, distorted my image, depicting me as a "Right winger at a press conference challenging a progressive *hijabi* Ilhan on a uniquely Muslim issue."

Whenever I speak publicly, I always introduce myself, who I am and whom I speak for. This was no different, especially, since I was wearing a sleeveless, navy-blue dress.

The truth was far from this portrayal; I wasn't a right-winger, it wasn't a formal press conference, and the problem of FGM extended beyond religious confines. This skewed narrative triggered a wave of hate from Ilhan's supporters on social media.

When the same media outlets started to see the public correcting their identification of who I was on what was then

Twitter, they started tweaking their articles. One progressive media outlet interviewed me to get my perspective, but the editor killed the story. Except for The Atlantic, any attempt to get the real story about FGM in America out was squashed.

Simultaneously, right-wing media seized the opportunity to vilify Ilhan, painting her as a radical sympathizer of FGM due to her deflection during our interaction. In this particular scenario, I was a convenient tool for the right-wing media.

This experience was a firsthand and hard lesson in media manipulation.

In the intricate dance between media biases and government-orchestrated events, I found myself questioning the purpose of a significant conference in 2019. The stage was set for the "Global Exchange on Religion in Society," a one-day event presided over by Federica Mogherini, who was both the High Representative of the European Union for Foreign Affairs and Security Policy, and Vice President of the European Commission. The gathering boasted 150 attendees from across the globe, representing diverse backgrounds, faith and non-faith perspectives, alongside European politicians and academia.

For a secular institution, they sure spent a lot of money on this one-day event. The conference included exchanging ideas through various breakout sessions, one of which I was asked to moderate and from which to report back to the larger plenary. The purpose of the conference was to inform attendees of this new Global Exchange platform, yet to be developed.

Yes, the conference was to launch an idea. What a luxury…

However, beneath the surface, the conference served a dual purpose—to launch an idea and, by extension, shape a narrative. To support the narrative, two EU-funded public policy briefs, "Building an EU International Exchange Platform on Religion and Social Inclusion," highlighted the need for positive narratives through an exchange platform.

The second was "Islam, Diversity, and Context" published by The Lokahi Foundation and funded by the European Union. Of course, we Muslims got "special" attention as other faiths didn't have their own brief! What was interesting about this policy brief was that, in the American context, it focused narrowly on neo-salafi and traditional institutions, and around Muslim-centric issues like "Islamophobia" and anti-Muslim attitudes, while omitting the plethora of other social issues we care about, such as the environment, women's and girls' and LGBTQ+ rights. This policy brief published in 2019 completely omitted the progressive attitudes of American Muslims.

It partially quoted statistics published by Pew Research Center's (PEW) studies on the attitudes of American Muslims in 2007 only, although subsequent statistics on the same set of questions were published in 2013 and 2017. The policy brief omitted PEW's statistics in the subsequent years, the positive change of attitudes of American Muslims on LGBTQ+ rights, and our support for critical thinking in theology, which proved that American Muslims are overwhelmingly progressive.

For example, in 2007, only 27 per cent of American Muslims supported LGBTQ+ rights; in 2017, it was 57 per cent. In recent years, this number is over 60 per cent. On the question of "should traditional understandings of Islam need to be reinterpreted to address modern issues," in 2017, 52 per cent of American Muslims responded affirmatively. In most Muslim-majority countries, this number is in single digits. And the most remarkable revelation is that 69 per cent of American Muslims say they pursue their spiritual life primarily outside the mosque. I count myself as one of them.

The omission of positive change in attitudes in the 2017 statistics in the policy brief, published in 2019, spoke volumes—an insidious suggestion that the dismal numbers in 2007 underscore that we, as Muslims, remain an intolerant enclave incompatible with the society we call home. The question was why?

I pondered if this was an intentional oversight or a ploy to perpetuate non-existing problems, or to ignore viable solutions? It seemed as if the proven solutions we have in America to creating societal cohesion were deliberately left out. Perhaps, in the realm of policymaking, perpetual problems ensure perpetual funding. Sometimes, I think policymakers and funders don't really want to solve the problems because that requires change, and if successful, they would have outgrown their usefulness.

When Trump got elected in 2016, conservative Muslim institutions floundered in their identity. The organization Council on American-Islamic Relations (CAIR) even reached out to me, sending a young male envoy to test the waters for a possible collaboration. CAIR and MPV have hardly been on the same side on most issues.

As a progressive woman who has always been critical of the positions CAIR has taken over the years particularly on women and LGBTQ+ rights, I found the outreach amusing. The way I saw it, it was because of organizations like CAIR, which have dominated the media landscape with their ultra-conservative position on social issues and with their homogenous definition of what and how a Muslim should be, that have resulted in the misinformation about Islam and Muslims. For years, CAIR's theological stance has been "Homosexuals are condemned," "Muslim women must wear hijabs," and "Music is forbidden." These positions are an Islam alien to the one I, and millions of others were raised on.

In America, the rise of these conservative institutions and religious leaders was funneled by Saudi funding at its inception, masquerading as the only true Islam, and was driven more by political expediency than genuine belief. The continued Saudi cultural colonization of the Muslim world and Muslims in the West has exacerbated the "us against them" dichotomy.

With their insistence that ultra-orthodox Islam is the only "true" Islam, it is easy for anti-Muslim champions to insinuate that all Muslims are the same, focusing on its perceived incompatibility with American values and democracy, and that they should therefore be deported. Trump only tapped into this well-established hate when he promised a "Muslim ban" on his campaign trails. Once in office, he banned travelers and refugees from mostly Muslim-majority countries: Iran, Iraq, Libya, Somalia, Sudan, Syria, and Yemen, and North Korea. This executive order was implemented supposedly in the name of security.

I am proud to be on the record to call Trump "a scumbag for riding on the misery of refugees" to win elections, and on Fox's Sean Hannity Show.

It is remarkable how Trump used the same hate-filled play-book again, this time demonizing illegal immigrants as rapists and criminals, and his use of the word "Palestinian" as a slur. Trump utilized prejudice and hate to win the election in 2024. It is an appalling reflection of our society.

As I've said earlier, the narrative of hate is powerful and is richly funded. An outfit designated as a hate entity by the Southern Poverty Law Center is Pamela Gheller. Her $100,000 advertise-ment campaign in 2010 included an advertisement with the Metropolitan Transportation Authority (MTA), New York, with a message that "all adherents to Islam will eventually become murderous savages." It was hate speech, plain and simple, masquerading as "freedom of speech." On another advertise-ment, it read: "In any war between the civilized man and the savage, support the civilized man," with the caption: Support Israel, Defeat Jihad.

This, by the way, is the exact same hate language that Isareli's right-wing politicians use to describe Palestinians in their assault on Gaza starting in 2023.

In yet another ad, it read: "The punishment of homosexuality is the death penalty—leading Islamic cleric, Sheik Qaradawi, of the Muslim Brotherhood. That's his jihad, what's yours?"

To counter this advertisement, MPV bought ours, which ran on the OMNI Bus in San Francisco for one month at a cost of $1,000 and it reads: "Whether straight or gay, Allah loves us all."

I am not fully blaming orthodox Muslim beliefs for the bane of the discrimination we receive from the likes of Gheller. Haters will be haters, but Muslims become an easy target when statements by religious leaders go unchallenged, giving the right-wing fodder.

Since the advent of Trump 1.0 and Trumpism, it was amusing to watch the conservative imams and religious leaders in America who for years scorned MPV's values all of sudden identify themselves as "progressives." By doing so, they were able to buy the safe cover of the secular progressive political Left at a time when the government was instituting discriminating practices against its own Muslim population.

In the Valley in Los Angeles County, at an annual march organized by the Interfaith Solidarity Network against racist hate and gun violence, to stand up for Justice, Peace, and Transformational Change, Rabbi Jim Kaufman invited me to sing a song. The song I sang was titled "In My Soul," lyrics adapted from Rabi'a al-Basri (717– 801 CE), a female Muslim Sufi saint and mystic from Iraq, and set to classical music, my original composition. Some of the lyrics are:

> "In my Soul there is a temple, shrine, a mosque, a church where I kneel.
> Prayer should bring us to an altar where no walls or names exist"

As we stood gathering at the end of the march, religious leaders took turns to make statements in reference to the theme of the event. One traditional imam declared, "We support women's rights and LGBTQ+ rights..."

I was eager to speak to him to learn in what way the mosque support LGBTQ+ rights, as we should work together! But he split the scene before everyone had their turn to talk.

So here's a bit of background and timeline.

During Trump's first term, the secular Left, including LGBTQ+ organizations, came to the defense of Muslims. Non-Muslims helped refugees settle, attorneys volunteered in droves at airports with international ports of entry for any Muslims who may have unfairly been detained by Immigration and Customs Enforcement (ICE) during the "Muslim Ban." Progressive churches, synagogues, and gay organizations rallied together in support of Muslims and mosques that became victims of hate crimes, which were plentiful.

Fast forward, upon winning the election, in 2021 President Biden signed an executive order undoing the "Muslim Travel Ban". Feeling safe, we saw the same conservative Muslim religious leaders "coming out" of their real closet, abandoning their fake progressive stance, and reverting back to their conservative, homophobic, and misogynistic positions.

In running MPV for the past 17 years, I have observed many cases filed and challenged by the religious Right, usually led by the Christian Right, challenging laws that they believe to inhibit their religious freedoms on matters of women's reproductive justice and LGBTQ+ rights. In opposition to these suits, I have contributed to numerous amicus briefs, or statements filed with the court, against the right to discriminate in the name of religion. MPV has become the go-to Muslim organization on matters of civil rights on abortion, LGBTQ+ and for the separation of church and state. We don't believe anyone should be allowed to be discriminated against in the name of religion. We've seen enough of that in many Muslim-majority countries.

In 2023, just as conservative Muslims started to intensify their partnership with the Christian right-wing coalition, the Israel-Hamas conflict flared up again, and along with it anti-Muslim and Islam rhetoric came back to center stage. For a minute, it made conservative Muslims reconsider their allyship with the Christian Right, until it became gainful at the expense of Palestinians.

To be manipulated by both the Left and the Right in the US political scene, the media, and to be used as a tool to get at each other as in the scenario with Congresswoman Ilhan Omar, I learned how hard it was to be calm and to be principled when under attack. In the Israeli-Hamas conflict, with so much violence and brutality exhibited, it is very hard to stand up for non-violence. It's not what many people want to hear. And for that, I've been "canceled" by some.

Too many Muslim organizations and religious leaders are fickle in their values. Whether I am "not Muslim enough" for some or "too Muslim" for others, I especially know that it is when there is tremendous pressure to concede, to bend to the powerful, or to go along with what is popular that standing up for your principles matters. It really does. It does not make for an easy path, but at least I can sleep at night.

***

# 6
# Power and empathy

All throughout life, I understood power. I understood it as a person raised in privilege, but through the prism of the poor. This was ingrained in me by what my parents would label as "educational trips" and the value of learning through exploration. My parents did not come from privilege and understood the importance of having values anchored in humility, ensuring that we never got *besar kepala*, meaning "big headed." These journeys were more than just geographical relocations; they were voyages of empathy, designed to broaden our perspectives and instill in us the profound responsibility that comes with privilege.

Back in those days, between the age of 6 and 12, when I was still allowed to be a kid, spanning the years between 1968 and 1974, my world expanded far beyond the familiarity of being chauffeured around, cared for by nannies, and cooks. It was a time when I would escape the bustling, privileged city life as an ambassador's daughter and dive headfirst into the heart of Malaysia as just another village girl in a small and clean neighborhood of Sungei Petani. This was where my mother's family resided. These months spent playing local games with my cousins, biking around the neighborhood, stopping over at neighbors' homes for a drink of water, getting candy at the neighborhood store on "credit", learning to sweep the floor, set the table, taking a cold bath with a bucket, learning to weave banana leaves for a sticky rice dish called *ketupat*, helped me connect with my Malay culture. It was also interesting for me to witness my grandmother living her life, her way.

My grandmother, Tok Wan, was married to a rich man. When she wanted fabric to be tailored into *baju kebaya*, an elegant traditional attire, the merchant would bring their latest and richest textiles to her home. When her rich husband expressed his desire to marry a second wife, she decided she didn't want to be part of that, and divorced him. This is a contrast to the experiences of many Muslim women today who are unable to secure a divorce.

She had 15 children and remained an independent and resilient woman who lived amidst life's hardships as a single parent, finding solace in simple pleasures like her beloved Coca-Cola. My mother would nostalgically recall how Tok Wan would sneak out of bed at night to the kitchen for a sip of Coke even in her last days. She lived to be 96 years old, healthy, strong, active, and determined till the day she died.

My mom used to say when I was younger that I am like my grandmother Tok Wan, "always busying yourself, never sitting still." I, like her, am always up and about, individualistic in nature, and determined to do things my way. As an example, when I was nine, I would call the doctor to make an appointment for myself, by passing my mother.

My mother married my father at the tender age of 16, and due to his successful occupation, Tok Wan benefited from my father's financial generosity. And with her many children contributing monetarily, my grandmother didn't live a life of poverty, and by Malaysian standards, that meant you had running water, a roof over your head, and a full belly.

At one time, Tok Wan had the only television in a few blocks, and so the neighborhood children, about 30 at least, sat in the living room. The young ones sitting on the lap of an elder sibling with every inch of the floor taken up and spilling to the front door to watch the afternoon cartoons (Photo: village kids at Grandma's). This communal sharing was filled with collective gasps, sighs, and laughter, and a contrast to my parents' home with our own family television room where it would usually just be my brother Malek and I being entertained.

**Figure 4:** Village kids at Grandma's

Then, when the afternoon shows were done, every single child thanked Tok Wan by kissing her hand before departing. The etiquette of thanking one's host was expressed differently from the one I was raised on, which was much more formal and Western in nature. Meanwhile, juxtapose that with the Los Angeles entertainment scene where people showed up late, crashed parties, and walked in and out of a house party as they pleased.

In 1970, and on one of my long summer breaks, I sometimes slept over for a few nights at my mother's sister, aunt Fazila's home in a poorer area of Sungei Petani where the streets were dirt roads, wooden houses perched on sturdy stilts placing the living space a good five feet above the ground, the steps leading up to the front door were just wooden planks without handrails, wooden panels around the house that opened up for natural light and for circulation of air, doubled up as walls when closed. Aunt Fazila's house was sparsely furnished with just a sofa and a coffee table, where my bed was just a mattress on the floor, and the toilet was an outhouse, essentially a hole in the ground. Despite the lack of modern amenities, this house had a television which we hardly watched as we were always playing. The lifeline to the outside world was one telephone in a phone booth down the street for the whole neighborhood to share. The village has, of course, changed with paved roads, the neighborhood phone booth deemed unnecessary with the advent of mobile phones.

One of the appealing things about Malaysia back then and now, are the local night markets or *pasar malam*. It resembles the American equivalent of a farmer's market. Farmers and village entrepreneurs would sell home prepared foods like fried noodles, *satay*, Malay desserts, tropical and local fruits in season and drinks like soybean or guava juice, and household items like steam pots, molds for making traditional dishes or flip flops. The smells, sights and sounds are uniquely Malaysian.

Back in the days, these night markets were not particularly clean, and the aftermath is usually a mess with piles of papers and plastics strewn around a large swath of ground. A few of my cousins would on occasion wake up before dawn before the city sent in their cleanup team to sift through the papers and plastics in search of money. So on one occasion I joined them. Witnessing their experience and joys of discovering some coins was a lesson that would stay with me throughout my life. Participating in their experience showed me the extent the poor go through for that extra dime, that opportunity to get ahead, that hustle. This too reflects how I pursue opportunities, leaving no stones unturned and especially as an immigrant and the underdog.

The experience also makes me go the extra mile to understand the context of the people I work toward lifting up today. For example, the exorbitant cost of internet connection in Burundi relative to how much it costs in America, and yet it's a utility that is necessary for you to even be heard, and therefore the hustle required just to be relevant.

Between 1969 and 1974, at the ages of 7 and 12, I lived in Egypt, and toward the end of the Arab-Israel war, a nation healing from its wounds became my classroom for understanding the ravages of conflict and the human toll it exacts.

One of the educational excursions was a trip my father organized with the Egyptian military to visit the city of Port Said after the Battle of Suez in 1973. To get to the city we first had to convene at the military base and from there we were escorted to Port Said City. I vividly recall the ride in the car with my dad, where the Malaysian flag fluttered, and a symbol of an official visit. Surrounded by a military escort, with police motorbikes leading the way both in front and at the back of our car, ensuring our safety so that we didn't wander off onto a road not cleared from landmines. And by the way, it is the responsibility of the host country to safeguard and protect its foreign diplomats, and this military escort was an example of such a treaty.

Port Said City was heavily destroyed in the war with Israel, the scars of war etched deeply into the landscape. I watched as the wind carried remnants of personal belongings—clothes and sheets—flapping like ghostly flags in the breeze, a haunting reminder of lives shattered by conflict. The once-intact apartment buildings were now sliced open by the brutal force of bombs, revealing the harsh reality of those who once called this place home. I couldn't help but wonder about the survivors, how many had made it out of the rubble that now covered half of the city.

During our visit, we jolted as we could hear the echoes of detonating bombs filling the air, a chilling sound that signified the Egyptian military's efforts to clear landmines, one explosive at a time. Strewn amidst the destruction were tanks, their formidable presence now reduced to mere wreckage. With the military's permission, my younger brother Malek climbed into one of these once-killing machines sitting on the barrel of the tank (Photo: Port Said City tank). I had, and still have an aversion to anything that symbolizes weapons of war and violence.

**Figure 5:** Port Said City tank

To witness the destruction, not just of buildings but of real lives buried beneath the rubble of geopolitical power struggles left a heavy emotional memory. Many decades later, I cannot help but feel the same grief that comes with seeing the thousands of homes and apartments bombed in Ukraine and Gaza, and in the case of Gaza the thousands of lives still buried under the rubble without the tools to dig out survivors. When the

Christian Palestinian pastor from Bethlehem, Dr Reverend Munther Isaac recreated the scene of the birth of baby Jesus, not in the manger as tradition has it, but as under the ruble to commemorate Christmas in 2023, it deeply resonated with me. It represented the burial of truth, the innocent under the weight of political corruption and power.

For me, this experience was more than just an encounter with the aftermath of war. It was a sobering realization of militarism's power and the inherent destructiveness it carried. This sentiment helped me identify, and name the discomfort I felt watching John Wane movies with Hollywood portrayals of dehumanized Native Americans, the gleeful arrogance of the cowboys mirroring the arrogance of those in power.

I hate violence and war. I attribute it to seeing its destruction first hand. I can't watch violent movies as it makes my stomach turn. And I hate injustice. It fills me with rage.

During these educational excursions, the dots of my understanding began to connect, weaving together a tapestry of values and beliefs that would shape the person I have become.

Due to the warring climate during our years in Egypt, from 1969 to 1973, the historical sites were all closed to tourism for security measures. The only historical site open for visitation was the Pyramids, which we could see from our balcony in the distance. We visited inside *Kuffu*, the largest of the three Pyramids, and regularly visited the site and the Sphinx to enjoy camel and donkey rides. This was my equivalent of Disneyland. However, my father decided this was not good enough, so he decided to coordinate a bus trip with the military just for the diplomats, including representatives from other countries, bringing them along to journey to Luxor. Such a community organizer! I must have gotten that from him.

While living in Cairo, my father, as ambassador to Lebanon, took my siblings and me to Beirut. This was the gateway for leisure, shopping, and entertainment for those residing in the Arab countries. Back then, it was the Paris of the Middle East. My family and I indulged in what seemed like a dreamy vacation—a few weeks of luxurious living in a hotel, soaking in the delights of sightseeing and endless hours by the pool. It was also the time that my late older brother Rahman taught me how to swim. But for my parents, mere leisure was never enough. There must always be an experience to learn from. One afternoon, they decided to transform our escapade into an educational journey, leading us to a Palestinian refugee camp.

As we stepped into the camp, a heavy sadness settled over me. Here were people displaced and discarded by the cruel hand of power, their dreams shattered, their self-empowerment stripped away. Lives were lost, futures were endlessly bleak. Even my poor cousins in Malaysia were much better off than the Palestinians. My family at least had the opportunity to make something out of their lives, they had the basic human right of freedom of movement and of dignity, while the Palestinians were deprived of such basic rights, hindered from pursuing their dreams and even if they did, no one was willing to give them an opportunity.

As I was a young girl, about 8 years old, in the family entourage to the refugee camp, we were followed by a group of children, their eyes lit up at seeing me. I suppose foreign children rarely visited them. Among them was a girl my age who looked at me straight in the eyes, her gaze pierced through me, which

I still feel till today. I lowered my eyes to break her gaze. At that point, I was uncomfortable with myself. I felt so guilty, although I am sure that was not her intention. For much of the educational excursion, I retreated, keeping my head low, my eyes glued to the dirt path beneath my feet.

Unlike the girl, my clothes fit me, my hair was clean and neatly braided, I had a comfortable life to go home to, and a future ahead of me—privileges that suddenly felt like heavy burdens. Long after that day, I still carry the memory of her eyes, a constant reminder of the disparities in our lives.

These educational trips weren't just about social justice and politics. To be culturally educated, my parents exposed us to the broad spectrum of experiences the world had to offer. They were a mix of work, play, and a gastronomic adventure led by my dad. My dad was the "work hard and play hard" kind of guy, and he particularly enjoyed discovering new cuisines. As he was the social type, he had friends all over the world from whom he would get references from, and this was long before the internet, predating the convenience of TripAdvisor, or reviews off Google, or Yelp.

During our stay in Germany between 1964 and 1969, we immersed ourselves in the lively festivities of the Bavarian Beer Fest. Dad took us especially so we could partake in the joyful celebration. Until today, come Octoberfest, I remember sitting at the long wooden table with delicious roasted chicken, laughing with and at the joyful Germans, swaying to music and song and with huge mugs of beer in their hands.

We traveled to the mountains of Bavaria, where I got to experience the sport luge, a two-seater version with the son of my dad's friend. To commemorate the fun excursion, my mother bought my younger brother Malek and I Bavarian outfits. His was a pair of *lederhosen*, a leather dark green pants with a strap over the shoulder, and mine was a *dirndl*, a dark blue dress with a red apron (Photo: Ani in Bavarian dress).

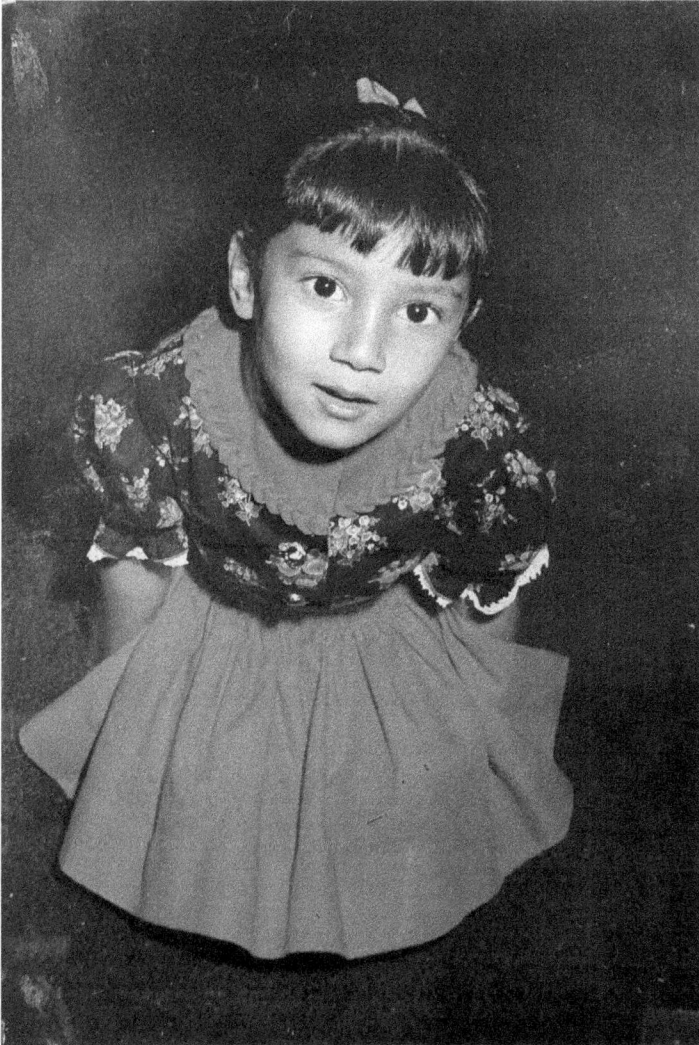

**Figure 6:** Ani in Bavarian dress

Living in India between the years 1974 and 1978, our travels spanned numerous cities and hillside towns, with stays at government-guest houses afforded to diplomats and funded by the Indian government. These residences resembled settings from classic British television shows depicting the last days of British colonization in India, such as "The Jewel in the Crown." The homes were expansive, elegant, and meticulously maintained. I distinctly recall our stay in the government guest house in Srinagar, the capital city of Kashmir. The way we were served and treated made me feel like the child of the last British Raja, with French service at the dinner table, where Western, not Indian, food was being served. The ambiance transported me to the bygone era of British rule, without the negative colonial experiences.

At the dinner table, my father got chatty with the servers, as usual asking them about the political situation, always wanting to learn and gaining insights into the political sentiments from the locals. It was clear even back then in the mid-70s, that Kashmiris harbored strong discontent with Indira Gandhi's governance of their province. Fast forward, we now see this discontent controlled with the militarization of Kashmir and the many human rights violations under Narendra Modi's Hindutva administration, a Hindu-supremacy ideology. It's not just in Kashmir, but nationally, religious minorities namely Muslims, Christians, and Sikhs are discriminated against with a multitude of human rights violations hardly reported in the Western media. Instead of condemning the myriad of discriminating policies, President Biden welcomes Modi with an official State visit. It is therefore hypocritical to call ourselves the torch bearer for human rights. The average world population pays close attention to world affairs more than the average American does. Our values are judged by this State dinner and whatever the American government does and does not do. Trustworthy is not one of those values.

Having met Indira Gandhi in person at a Malaysian independence reception, where I shook her hand, I was well aware of her
extreme political stance (Photo: Indira Gandhi). I had lived under
her Emergency rule as a teenager, and it was like living behind
an iron curtain. I had experienced the prohibition of all things
foreign, whether they be foreign products, pop music, or cultural influences. On the radio and TV, all you heard was classical
Indian *raga* music and dance. The Western-infused Bollywood
music we have today did not exist back then. If you wanted anything Western, you would have to go to the American Embassy
Commissary. It was there that I watched *Jaws*, ate a burger and
fries. To get caught up with the outside world, every time my
international friends came back from their summer vacations,
they would come back with records and teen magazines. It was
my window into the world of pop culture I was missing, which
made me look forward to leaving and experiencing the rest of
the world outside and beyond the metaphorical iron curtains.

**Figure 7:** Indira Gandhi

Reflecting on history, Gandhi's policy to control population growth coerced millions of men into sterilization, a practice I find objectionable. Just as I wouldn't want enforced pregnancy on anyone in my advocacy work today, I certainly wouldn't support forced sterilization either. It led me to ponder what the servers at that Indian government guest house might have thought if they knew we had shaken her hand, the same clenched-fisted hand in the manner she ruled India. I think, being Malaysian and Muslim, they trusted my father enough to share their truth. And, interestingly enough, in my human rights work today, I make sure to mention I'm originally from Malaysia and a Muslim, because as an American, it is hard to gain trust.

Through all these educational excursions, my parents never uttered anything derogatory or expressed prejudice toward anyone or about any party within a conflict. Whether they had any strong feelings or not, it was never shared. It helped me grow up without prejudice. It is for this reason that I found the speech I heard by Louis Farakhan to be unpalatable.

Many decades later, in November of 2017, I got to go on an educational excursion—an invitation from American Jewish Committee's Project Interchange to visit Israel and Ramallah in Occupied Palestine, as part of a delegation of American Muslim leaders. Our trip included visiting various sites in Jerusalem, Ramallah, Tel Aviv, and from there, a 20 minute helicopter ride to the Golan Heights bordering Syria. We met with high-ranking Israeli government officials, as well as the two women who founded a 50,000-member Israeli-Palestinian Women Wage Peace group that in 2016 organized a march to pressure the

Israeli government to negotiate peace with the Palestinians. We also had a long morning visit at the residence of an Israeli Palestinian sharia court judge, Kadi Mohamad Abu Ubied, and in the occupied West Bank, we met with Palestinian Authority's Prime Minister Rami Hamdallah at his office, and the Palestinian-American entrepreneur Bashar Masri.

There were many highlights I could share about the trip but there are a few that stood out.

We traveled as a group in a comfortable bus with a tour guide and driver, both Israeli Jews. Instead of sitting in the back in the passenger seat, I chose to sit up front beside the tour guide to ask him questions in between the official "tour narrative." I found out that he was once a policeman. He pointed out signs in Hebrew that mandated dress code for women, and quickly disclosed that he was an atheist. He shared how Orthodox Jews don't pay taxes, have large families and can exempt themselves from serving in the army to defend Israel, whereas it is compulsory for everyone else. I could tell he didn't care much for the Orthodox Jews. At that point, we got to discuss how ultra-Orthodox Jews and Orthodox and conservative Muslims share many of the same religious traits.

I guess my inquisitiveness must have made an impression on him, because years later I am told this tour guide asked about me.

I pointed out Hebrew signs that passed us by for him to translate. One stated that permits were required for Jews to enter Arab areas. Some observations didn't require any translations, though. Driving through various neighborhoods and on the helicopter ride from Tel Aviv to the border with Syria, it was clear which enclaves belonged to Israeli Jews and which were Arab-Israeli, or rather, Palestinian. Jewish neighborhoods were well maintained and lush with trees and shrubs because they had an unlimited supply of water, whereas the Palestinian neighborhoods were just barren, dilapidated with un-repaired street lights and, well, grim. It was as if we were in a different country and it was clear which community had preferential treatment. The grimness reminded me of my trip from West Germany to Berlin in East Germany decades ago, where the landscape changed from lush to gray and, well, depressing.

One thing to note is how Palestinians were called Israeli Arabs. They are Palestinians, but if Israelis are to call them Palestinians, it would validate the existence of a nationality, Palestine. By calling Palestinians "Israeli-Arabs" it intentionally erases an identity. This is a classic colonial modus operandi. Palestinian Jews, or Arab Jews, who are also indigenous to the land switched their identity to Israel upon the creation of the State. Regardless of country, one's identity— whether it be race, religion, or tribe, has always been used to manipulate the population, a political chip, pitched against each other by giving preferential treatment of one over the other. The remarkable thing is the general population always falls for the divide-and-conquer ruse. Look at how prolific President Trump was at vilifying one group over another.

Praying at the al-Aqsa Mosque for a Friday prayer was part of the itinerary. That too was a high-security area. The group of us women in the tour group prayed outdoors on the plaza. It was a spiritual experience, the air laced with recitation in

Arabic, with church bells ringing in the background. The multireligious nature of Jerusalem can never escape you, faith—diverse and beautiful. It still makes me smile.

We also went to visit Mr. Mohammed Abu-Ubied, a judge at the Baka al Gharbiyye Sharia Court, at his home in Na'ura. I am particularly interested in how the State of Israel reconciles its Orthodox Judaism with its supposedly secular and democratic label. In my opinion, it is not possible to be both a democratic and theocratic state. Theocracy, by definition, favors one religion above all others, which the State of Israel does. It was therefore interesting for me to speak to a sharia court judge about how that fits into Israel's democratic but Jewish state identity.

I learned so much from Mr. Abu-Ubeid. The religious courts—Muslim, Christian, and Orthodox Judaism rule everyday peoples' lives. Conservative, Reform, Constructionist Judaism are not recognized in Israel. As a Muslim judge, he uses the most liberal *mazhab* (denomination) values to adjudicate cases on matters of family law. I asked him about interfaith marriages, and he noted that Muslim women marrying non-Muslim men is starting to become an issue. He also shared that upon the creation of Israel, the British-controlled Islamic charity institutions, or *waqf,* and its assets were turned over to Israel, whereas assets of the Church were returned to the Church. Such was the unfair treatment of the British government. The British betrayal of the Palestinians and their hand in settling European Jews in Palestine is a source of world conflict till today. This is parallel to the erasure of the indigenous people of North America in its colonization and in creating a new, "White" nation, the United States of America.

When entering the West Bank, we crossed a check point where, armed with machine guns, women and men came on board to look us and our passports over. One of the machine guns almost brushed against my shoulder, and it was unsettling. Once we were on the other side of that checkpoint, we had to switch buses to get on a Palestinian-registered bus with Palestinian driver and tour guide to the West Bank. Our Israeli driver and tour guide stayed at the checkpoint and waited for our return back to Israel.

This was our first visit to a new neighborhood, Rabawi, developed by Bashar Masri, a wealthy Palestinian American from New Jersey. His property development of 5,000 apartment units included an outdoor Greek theater for live performances and entertainment, a shopping area, cafes and restaurants, and even a hiking trail. The walls of the Greek theater were decorated with murals of famous Palestinian singers and cultural icons, to reinforce its cultural heritage. The road leading into Rabawi was what I would describe as one lane of the 101 freeway in Los Angeles. It is wide enough for one truck to drive through. Why do you ask? Because that was all the Israeli authority would allow. In other words, even with the tremendous willpower to build and create a life for Palestinians, the Israeli made sure it was not going to be easy.

Mr. Masri sat down for coffee with us, sharing how he almost lost his investment to bankers when the Israeli government would not turn the water on to the property development. Yes, the issue of water is noticeable. In the Occupied Territories, the Israeli government rations the amount of water allowed to Palestinians. The apartment units were all completed, units sold, but the taps ran dry. Through sheer determination shuttling between various Israeli departments, the Israeli authorities finally allowed water to flow through.

The one who controls water, the sustenance for life, is where power is. This is not just an issue in Israel-Palestine, it is a global issue, and here in the US it is a battle among the states that flourish from water of the Colorado River.

Funny enough, our next stop was a trip to meet with a high-ranking Israeli government official in Jerusalem. He talked for about ten minutes about how it was important for the Palestinians to build up their own economy, and then he paused and said, "Feel free to interrupt because we here in Israel like to engage in debate." So I interrupted him.

I challenged him on his point with, "How can Palestinians develop their economy when you have only allowed for a one-lane road for this massive property development, and refused access to water?"

He was taken aback and responded with the default response, "it's security issues."

Yes, water is a security issue as it provides sustenance. Sustenance of the Palestinian people is not what the politicians of Israel want. This was glaringly illustrated with the bombing of water-purifying facilities in Gaza in 2024.

Another noteworthy moment was meeting an Israeli peace negotiator between Israel and Jordan. He was a hard-nosed older man and an atheist. At dinner, he opened up and shared a personal story, an experience with his son that he didn't anticipate. For privacy reasons I will call him Mr. Negotiator. Incidentally, it should be noted at how secular and atheist Israeli Jews openly identify themselves as such without any prompts. It almost feels as if they see themselves superior over Orthodox Jews.

Mr. Negotiator and his son, who was 12 years old at that time, went hiking near their home in Tel Aviv. They brought a camera along with them, taking photos from a hilltop. Then a group of four young Palestinian youths came up the hill, also to enjoy the outdoors and the view. Mr. Negotiator felt his son's discomfort, so they hiked back down. As they almost reached the bottom of the hill, one of the Palestinian young men ran with something in hand, holding it up in the air, calling out, "Mister, mister!" They turned around, his son frozen in fear. The Palestinian youth said, "You left your camera lens cover".

Mr. Negotiator disclosed that he was very careful to not create an environment of prejudice at home, but he realized that the outside world had overpowered and successfully infused prejudice of Palestinians onto his son. In his tone, I could tell he was saddened by that defeat.

It was a sobering moment. I was deeply touched by his honesty and got teary-eyed. In preparation of meeting someone new, I always read the person's biography or CV in hopes that we may have a shared interest to help strike up a conversation with. I was not expecting such an exchange. Yes, I am sure he is a tough bargainer, but he was also a father, and a human being. We all have our vulnerabilities.

In my dealings with government officials and diplomats, I'm lucky to work with people who share my values, and, in this case, who do what they can to support the livelihood of Palestinians and Gazans. In the current political climate there is much disdain for Western democracies worldwide for their unapologetic support of Israel's current genocide of Palestinians. It is also important to point out that we should not generalize, and that there are allies even within these governmental institutions.

Before 2017, farmers in Gaza weren't able to easily sell their produce, as trucks were held up at checkpoints along various Gaza-Israel security fences for long periods, resulting in the produce rotting away in the sun. The reason? Israel's position is, "It's a security issue, as there could be bombs in the trucks." To overcome this security concern, on behalf of the government of the Netherlands, Ambassador Roderick Van Schreven negotiated a solution with the Israeli government, which resulted in the purchasing and placement of several drive-through X-ray machines that scan trucks for their contents, thus easing Israeli's security concerns and providing an income stream for Gazan farmers.

When one entity operates from the perspective of insecurities, then it tends to function out of fear in the guise of control. Whether an individual or a nation-state, the treatment of "the other" will be inhumane. These insecurities play out in our politics, policies, and right down to family dynamics, resulting in social injustice and human rights violations. Control appears in the form of power, and the ugliness of that power is the inability to empathize. We all have our insecurities, and, therefore, we all have that ugly side.

At this point in my life, I've had friends of all nationalities. Within our interfaith settings, Jews, Christians, Muslims, Buddhists, Hindus—we all get along, and, more importantly, show up for each other. A Cantor I know puts on a magnificent interfaith musical event with diverse representations at his synagogue. It usually includes a choir from an African-American church, an Islamic call to prayer, and occasionally, I would join the interfaith choir in this annual celebration of Dr Martin Luther King, Jr.'s birthday in January. At the heart of Dr King's message was nonviolence, but somehow, with the heinous attack on Israel by Hamas in October 2023, and with the slaughter of innocent Palestinians, majority of whom are children as punishment at the hands of Israel, all that pompous show about nonviolence rings hollow if you can't even utter the word "cease fire" or call for ending the Occupation.

Claiming to stand for the values of nonviolence in times of peace is too easy. What counts is when it is difficult and when it is directed at "the other", at the enemy. I have lost all respect for these superficial peace actors, and have gained a whole new level of respect for the true disciples of nonviolence— Dr King, Mandela, Reverend Desmund Tutu, and Ghaffar "Badshah" Khan. I intentionally left out Mahatma Gandhi due to his racism toward Black South Africans and prejudice against those in the lowest caste, dalit. Being prejudiced is a form of violence.

In observing the Palestinians, their perseverance to live is no different than that of the Israelis. Together these two peoples, should they one day live side by side as two nations, will excel, and they can accomplish so much as partners rather than as enemies. Together they hold the keys to a more peaceful world. As a hopeless optimist, I believe the establishment of a Palestinian statehood is inevitable.

Living in countries like Egypt and India, the stark contrast between my life and the harsh realities of absolute poverty became painfully evident. During my time in New Delhi, between 12 to 16 years old, I fell into the complex social hierarchies of the nation, a society deeply entrenched by the corrosive effects of the caste system. As an outsider, I witnessed the blatant discrimination faced by the *dalits*, the marginalized "untouchables." This eye-opening experience served as a poignant precursor, sensitizing me to the deeply entrenched caste prejudices that had also infiltrated American society.

In New Delhi, our residence was within the Malaysian government's compound, housing the embassy, the ambassador's residence, and homes for the servants managing the property. Even within this microcosm, the stark disparities of caste were glaringly apparent. Our in-house helper, a tall, dark man who hardly smiled, belonged to a higher caste, contrasted sharply with our outdoor helper, a *dalit*, who no matter how hot or cold the weather was, always carried a smile. He was in charge of up-keeping the large grounds as the *chaukidar* (gardener). Although both of them lived in the same living spaces in the servant's quarters of the Malaysian compound, our butler's prejudiced mentality manifested in his refusal to share a cup or eat from the same plate as our gardener. He went to great lengths to separate his cups, plates, and utensils, positioning them high in the kitchen cabinet to keep them separate from the rest. Rejecting this divisive attitude, my mom made a deliberate effort to ensure that both our helper and gardener witnessed us using the same set of plates and utensils as the gardener, making the point that discrimination is not tolerated through our simple yet symbolic action. By Ibram X. Kendi's definition, this was our proactive stance as anti-racists.

I vividly recall an incident when my mother informed me about chatter circulating regarding my soccer drills (or football for the rest of the world) with the son of our *dalit* servant, and how "inappropriate" that was. Her response was resolute, "Don't be bothered by it. Continue to play." This simple, yet powerful, statement became a guiding light, teaching me to stand against prejudice even when it is the norm.

Beyond the confines of our compound in New Delhi, I witnessed abject poverty. During my school commute, as I rode comfortably in our chauffeured Mercedes, I witnessed families residing in makeshift homes constructed from recycled materials on vacant plots. For our always-smiley Nepalese driver, Ramzy, the scene was normal, while, for me I watched in agitated silence. Children, oblivious to their nakedness, played in the dirt while their mothers cooked amidst meager resources, utilizing patties of cow dung both as fuel and to reinforce the walls of their humble abodes. These scenes etched themselves into my consciousness, adding to the layers of life's lessons and observations, the building blocks to a lifelong of empathizing, and the springboard to challenging societal injustices.

Regrettably, the insidious caste system has found a foothold in the United States. Despite the hopes of those who emigrated to America, the specter of caste-based discrimination continues to haunt personal and professional spheres, notably within the American tech industry. Disturbing incidents, such as emails exposed urging managers not to hire workers from the *dalit* caste, highlights the persistence of this discrimination within some Indian emigrants. In response, concerted efforts have been made to combat this injustice.

At MPV in California, we collaborated with progressive organizations like Hindus for Human Rights to advocate for the inclusion of castes as a protected category in the bill SB 403 within the state's civil rights law, alongside race and sex. One would think, considering the American ethos of "justice for all," this effort would be a breeze, but instead, this fight was arduous, marked by bitter opposition well-funded by the advocacy group Hindu American Foundation, which is dominated by upper-class Hindus who are doing the discrimination. I want to highlight the unwavering courage of State Senator Aisha Wahab, who stood firm against pressures from Hindutva forces, even while receiving death threats. Her resilience exemplifies the strength needed to challenge deeply entrenched biases and fight for a more just society. Sadly, though, in 2023, Governor Gavin Newsom vetoed the bill.

There's more to this than this short paragraph, but I bring it up as a correlation of how my upbringing and awareness of the caste prejudices I experienced in India has informed and sensitized me to this issue here and now. How an Indian immigrant of a lower caste is discriminated against has no impact on my life, but it is important to show up for the rights of others.

Beneath the surface of poverty and conflict lies the intricate web of power dynamics, dividing the world into the haves and the have-nots. These divisions manifest through various lenses, such as class, race, nationality, or religion. Among these, race and religion stand out as particularly potent forces, shaping and solidifying one's sense of identity. It is when these shared identities are pitted against one another, leading to notions of superiority or inferiority, that racism and prejudice flourish. This collision of identities deepens the divide, fostering an environment ripe for discrimination and bias to take hold.

In the vibrant mosaic of my adolescence, I found myself in London, facing racial prejudice firsthand. The ignorant words of a child labeling us as "coloreds" were a stark reminder of the prejudices that plague even the most cosmopolitan of cities.

On a short vacation in London, I was hanging out with friends from the Malaysian diplomatic core, and we went to a neighborhood park. Other than two children on a swing and on the slide, the park was empty. Upon entering the park premises, the older boy said to his sibling "Come on let's go, the coloreds are here".

"What is a colored?" I asked, because at about seven years old, I was pretty naïve.

My friend, who was older than I, responded, "It means we're brown, and that's why they didn't want to play with us and left".

"That's too bad. Well, we now have the whole place to ourselves!" I said.

Having a positive disposition has helped me overcome tremendous hurdles in adulthood. In that moment, it hurts, and sometimes it is hard to overcome negativity and discrimination, and particularly the back-stabbing. It is therefore best to sit with yourself and to strategize on how to overcome the odds. Sitting with yourself means tuning out the world. I contemplate what I want to accomplish, the steps I need to take to get there, and, most importantly, the discipline required in every moment spent toward my goals. With each step, I feel proud of myself, and success, as they say, is the sweetest revenge.

As I was being instilled with empathy, as you know, I was also being groomed to carry myself "properly" around the powerful. From an early age, I was introduced to Presidents, Prime Ministers and government officials.

While I was absorbing these cultural and prejudicial issues on a micro level, I was very drawn to foreign policy. By the age of 11 years old, I was reading my father's copy of the Far Eastern Economic Review. With its very complicated English vocabulary, I would have a dictionary next to me. Through the Review, I would absorb the politics of the Vietnam War, distinctively remembering the magazine cover of a naked girl about my age running, a victim of an American napalm bomb, screaming in pain, amongst other in-depth foreign policy coverage. I also remember reading about US Aid, and I commented to my father, "Americans are very generous!" to which my father said, "Nothing comes for free Ani, be careful of the strings attached." I remember that lesson until today.

In every encounter, in every challenge, I am reminded of the words my father spoke to me years ago, cautioning me about the strings attached with giving. Those strings may pull, but I also have the power to pull the string back in the direction that I want. Above all, relationships, whether business or personal, are about how stakeholders can mutually benefit in that relationship. Pulling the string too hard will break it. I have found it best to be moderate, to give and take, and to be mindful of the other person's needs and desires. When you recognize the other person's human dignity, even the oppressors', the person will likely recognize that in you as well. If they don't, then that is probably not someone you want to have in your life, whether that be a personal or a business relationship. You will go further in life leveraging negativity with a positive attitude, and, not to mention, you will become a happier person.

My experiences of leveraging the validity of my work in human rights in an effort to appeal for funding have been challenging. For the first seven years, I spent my own time and resources building MPV. Launched in a toxic anti-Muslim climate, and wedged between being too Muslim and not Muslim enough, it was hard to be heard, and, therefore, relevant.

In years 8 through 17 of MPV, the work became very visible in the US and internationally and the framing in how we implement our advocacy has been duplicated by progressive Muslims in other countries like Argentina, Brazil, Canada, the UK, Germany, Italy, and France. For example, by highlighting the fact that marriage in Islam is between two adults of sound mind and that the woman's permission to marry is required, we are able to counter the justification for child or forced marriages. By making the English writings of progressive theologians and philosophers accessible to the general public at a middle school level, we are able to reach a broad audience through social media, bypassing the religious authorities, meaning, bypassing power.

Despite the proven track record of the effectiveness of our human rights advocacy, raising funds to scale up our programs was always a challenge. I apply to foundations and although successful in one year, there is no guarantee the support will continue in subsequent years. Most foundations will fund you for one year, maybe two, and, if you're very lucky, for three years, and they expect miracles. The power of their purse is palpable. For a long time, funders were very stingy with how much of their funding is allowed to pay for operational expenses like salaries, insurance, or bills to turn the lights on! Somehow, it was and for some, still are oblivious that it costs money to run an organization that supports the implementation of the programming. Needless to say, it took me many years to learn the ropes of how to create a budget. Small nonprofits are not taught how to create a budget, and, therefore, for many—especially women leaders—we tend to do things for free. And we are taken advantage of for it.

In recent years though, since Black Lives Matter and the killing of George Floyd, funders are much more sensitive to the well-being of change-makers, resulting in some even allowing for nonprofits to add a budget line for self-care. After many years of grant writing and fundraising, I'm learning that the most dependable resource is to create your own income stream.

Unlike funding from foundations, the power dynamics of donations from individuals is tricky. For some context, usually big checks from individual donors come with strings attached such as having a college department or the name of a building named after them. People give for a cause they care about—a cancer research organization because a close loved one died of cancer, or the YMCA because they grew up underprivileged and it was the YMCA that provided them with free sports facilities when they were young, or a religious institution you are affiliated with. In general, not always, individual donors tend to serve their self-interest, and they will only give to an issue or a cause that benefits them, or one they have an emotional connection with.

As a woman soliciting donations for a cause, I have had the unfortunate experience of dealing with unscrupulous men, because, well, it only benefitted them. And, of course, just like my father taught me; "Be careful of the strings attached."

Yes, even in the effort of making the world a better place, women still endure sexual harassment. As the #MeToo movement has identified womenfolk seeking opportunities in the entertainment business, and just about every industry, have experienced uncomfortable situations and violations of the worst kind. Power dynamics come in different forms. Regardless of whether it is the entertainment industry, religion, or even human rights, power and exploitation is a constant thread.

In navigating the turbulent waters of prejudice and discrimination, I draw strength from the resilience of my grandmother,

Tok Wan, whose unwavering independent spirit defied social norms by divorcing her husband and parenting as a single mom in an era when that was taboo. I draw inspiration from the diverse tapestry of my childhood friends who taught me that true friendships transcend the boundaries of religion, race and nationality. And I draw courage from the lessons of my parents, who instilled in me the profound understanding that with privilege comes an even greater responsibility—to challenge the status quo, dismantle prejudices, and pave the way for a more inclusive world. And, to do that, I had to learn how to empathize, and most importantly, to identify the powers that try all they can to prohibit us from empathizing with each other.

***

# 7
# The liars and the truth-tellers

Growing up, my parents never held back in their admonitions: "Ani, think before you open your mouth," they would say, or, "Ani, God gave you brains, use them!" I couldn't deny it—I was a chatterbox, a fact that my teachers never failed to mention in my report cards.

However, it wasn't until college that I truly took their advice to heart. Now, in my current work, I meticulously weigh every word I utter or write, considering its accuracy, truthfulness, and, above all, its fairness. The wisdom of my parents' words became crystal clear to me.

One of the fundamental teachings of the Quran emphasizes the seeking of knowledge and fostering critical thinking, which was what my parents had been hammering into me. I find it interesting that my parents' advice to me wasn't made into a religious duty but one from rationality and responsibility in order for me to be my best self, which is the prerequisite to serving humanity effectively. Ironically, despite this crucial teaching, many Muslim-majority countries that claim to be "Islamic" are the worst implementers of this teaching. Their Muslim population in general, and yes, you guessed it, especially women and girls, often lag behind in literacy. This discrepancy serves as a poignant reminder of the work that still needs to be done to ensure equal access to education for all.

Reflecting on the teachings of the Qur'an, I can't help but question why the Muslim world finds itself in such a pitiful state, drowning in poverty and plagued by limited opportunities and violence. The answer is the politicization of Islam. Keeping the masses uneducated and impoverished makes them easier to control, and an endless supply of cheap labor like caregivers, private drivers, housekeepers, gardeners, etc. Even businesses are able to keep the cost of their employees' labor extremely low, directly resulting in larger profits margins for the business owners. This social hierarchy, regardless of Muslim or not, carefully engineered, serves the interests of the rich and powerful. This is vividly evident in Gulf countries where importation of the poor for cheap labor forms the backbone to the servicing industry, the development of mega-projects, and in maintaining their lavish lifestyle. This income gap is also stark in countries like India and Pakistan, and in America that gap has widened, which, in my opinion, is the making of a failed state or a dysfunctional democracy at best.

Religious authorities, not just in Islam but in most religions, tend to weave their narratives, claiming to possess the ultimate truth while promoting a specific agenda, a one-sided perspective. Religious authorities and institutions that peddle an oppressive interpretation of "Islam, " or any religion for that matter, are designed to benefit the political and economic elites. This strategy is as old as the creation of religion. The Romans adopted Catholicism, and boy did they rule, and brutally too—enriching themselves and benefiting from it to this day.

In the Muslim world, some religious leaders, paradoxically, present themselves as advocates of peace on global platforms like the United Nations and the European Union. It baffles me how these self-proclaimed leaders, often funded with millions of dollars by the affluent Gulf States, organize and host flashy, extravagant international interfaith conferences while perpetuating the very issues that they claim to fight against. The hypocrisy is staggering.

In the past decade, a slew of so-called "declarations," like the Marrakesh Declaration and the Fez Declaration, has flooded our awareness. The Marrakesh Declaration produced on January 27, 2016, pledges equal treatment of non-Muslims in Muslim-majority countries. The last paragraph reads:

"Call upon representatives of the various religions, sects and denominations to confront all forms of religious bigotry, vilification, and denigration of what people hold sacred, as well as all speech that promote hatred and bigotry; and finally, affirm that it is unconscionable to employ religion for the purpose of aggressing upon the rights of religious minorities in Muslim countries."

What is galling about this declaration is its redundancy. These principles are presented as if they are an epiphany of an "enlightened" group of Muslim religious leaders. These principles are, in fact, nothing new. They were written down as agreements and implemented by Prophet Muhammad in the Medina Constitution and the Covenants with Christians and Jewish tribes in the 700s. The glaring gap is between this centuries-old covenant and its absence in the education of Muslim communities today.

Even after signing on to this declaration, its signatories, consisting of heads of Muslim governments and prominent religious leaders, continue to violate their pledge. Take, for instance, Pakistan, where Christians and Hindus are perse-cuted, and Christian girls are forced to convert to Islam when marrying a Muslim man. In Iran, Baha'is are still unjustly treated. All these are un-Islamic practices and this subject matter deserves a book unto itself.

The principle behind crafting the Marrakesh Declaration is Sheikh Abdallah bin Bayyah originally from Mauritania. While he's on the world stage, touted as an iconic religious leader promoting human rights, his countryman Mohamed Cheikh Ould Mkhaitir, a Mauritanian blogger, was sentenced to death by the sharia court for apostasy on December 25, 2014. He was imprisoned for five years in horrible conditions and for those five years the United Nations, human rights advocates, including myself, campaigned for his release. I am happy to share he now lives in France, is married, and has a child.

You see, interfaith work is easy. It is outward-looking. Religious figures camouflage themselves by using human rights lan-guage, and people will put them in the "good" column. People won't question what you do WITHIN your community, because honestly, people don't care.

In general, Christian and Baha'i organizations are absolutely thrilled to have a Muslim religious leader like Bayyah address the prejudice that their constituencies face in Muslim-majority countries, but in general, it is not their priority  if a Muslim is sentenced to death for speaking truth to power.

Interfaith communities should be questioning, supporting and partnering in how these declarations translate into pol- icies, Islamic curricula, and religious educational institutions that train imams and religious teachers are being churned out, and how is this implemented in educational programming in the most remote villages? What's the point of a declaration if there's no follow-through?

Can you imagine what a different Muslim world we would be in if we were taught about the Medina Constitution and the Covenants from a young age in all our religious schools? In my effort to generate this change, I co-created the Inclusive Islam Curriculum, rooted in human rights values for children in the West, that included these historic, rights-affirming Covenants.

Similarly, this knowledge gap between theology and prac- tice isn't confined to Muslim-majority countries. It plays out in cities throughout the Western world. At interfaith marches and events, some imams of local mosques proclaim publicly with statements such as "We support women and LGBTQ+ rights" while they neglect to take ownership of this issue by promoting these values in their Sunday school curricula or Friday prayer sermons. Not a single word. Rather than nurture critical thinking they prefer blind conformity from their con- gregational members, and thus maintain that only they are qualified to interpret religion. They would lose their authority and power if they encouraged critical thinking and dissent, and they know that.

Traditional religious schools often suppress critical thinking, stifling questions about religion, God's existence, and the stories in the sacred texts. These institutions emphasize conformity, molding followers instead of nurturing leaders which is the common practice of madrassas (religious schools). Some of the children receive this religious education in an abusive and sometimes violent manner. In my own personal experiences, my daughter didn't escape this harmful style of teaching.

At the age of 4–6 years old, I enrolled my daughter at the local mosque's Sunday school, hoping she could build friendships with American Muslim kids, deeply imbued in their American identity, and diversify her pool of friends the way mine were growing up. It was a commitment for me as an engaged parent to take out a few hours of our Sunday for this effort. The curriculum appeared promising on paper. I liked it, but unfortunately the authoritative teaching style, reminiscent of my experiences in the Egyptian educational system, did not encourage child-centered learning. The teaching style in Los Angeles did not reflect the distance between Cairo and California!

On one occasion, my daughter, in her openness, shared with her teacher and classmates that she accidentally ate a ham sandwich at a friend's house. The teacher proceeded to tell her that she was going to hell. My daughter raised her hand and disputed this position by stating that, since it was an accident, she wouldn't go to hell. She was immediately ostracized and asked to stand in a corner.

The emphasis on hell is not the way religions should be taught. In this case, it should have been, "God loves you so much that you are allowed to eat pork if that is all you have to eat, for preservation of life is paramount."

In another incident, my daughter called out, "Mama, papa, I don't want to be a Muslim anymore because I'm afraid I'll go to hell for pushing a friend and hurting him."

That was the last straw. I pulled her out of Sunday school immediately. Regardless of religion, being imbued in love and the freedom to think freely is a better way to raise your child than that of fear.

My daughter's experience at her religious school was nothing compared to the abusive nature endured by millions of Muslim children. In most *madrassas* hitting the child's hand with a ruler for a mispronounced Arabic word or caning to discipline a child is the norm. In Burkina Faso, I was told a teacher put a scorpion in the hands of a child as punishment. This abusive manner is an exhibition of power and ego, both emotional and physical. This abusive and violent form of teaching, in my opinion, is why violence is rife in many Muslim societies.

Religious education should inspire love, compassion, and understanding, not fear and condemnation. Instead of nurturing curiosity and empathy, so many of these religious schools instill dread. Such an approach contradicts the essence of faith of lifting our spirits. There is an urgent need for a reformation in religious education to foster understanding, acceptance, and genuine spiritual growth.

***

A few years ago, my younger brother, Malek, joined the Tabligh movement, a particular teaching of Islam originating from India, emphasizing kindness, God-consciousness, and adherence to the "teachings of Prophet Muhammad." Nothing wrong with that. So far so good. However, the problem was that Tabligh teachings relied primarily on the *hadith*, a collection of writings compiled hundreds of years after the passing of the Prophet that documented his sayings and behaviorisms, some of which are clearly fabrications.

To emulate the Prophet, in the typical Tabligh movement dress code, my brother dresses like Prophet Muhammad. He wears a gray or beige robe, a long beard and sandals. His focus is on the Tabligh community only and proselytizing Muslims to their fold. They do not proselytize non-Muslims. He has also chosen to educate his two sons through secular elementary school only, and now, at the ages of 14 and 16, they attend a *madrassa*, have no choice but to be groomed in the Tabligh way of life, robe and all.

This Tabligh movement promotes living and taking on the behavior of Prophet Muhammad, regarding him as exemplary, which he is. To me, he exemplified the best moral values, through his exceptional kindness as reflected in his relationships with his wives, animals, and the environment—an image starkly different from the distorted portrayals of a pedophile that Right-wing Christians, Zionists, Hindutvas, and ex-Muslims make him out to be. He treated non-Muslims fairly and was rightfully furious when his co-religionists behaved unjustly. His life was a testament to hard work and family values; he lived for a good 22 years of his life, working for his wife Khadijah, a successful, thriving businesswoman, was a husband and father ever present and handy around the house, and actively participated in household chores including mending his own clothes. In modern language, we call this positive masculinity.

I attempted to reason with my brother, challenging his decision to deprive his sons, my nephews of a high school education, a decision that contradicts Prophet Muhammad's teachings, which advocated the pursuit of knowledge "Even if you have to go to China." Malek's response—that his sons didn't need formal education to earn a living because "God will provide for them"—made me angry.

Malek was the only sibling that was a constant in my life. We shared the same bedroom; as young children, we shared a bath together, playing with bubbles and rubber ducks. We went to the same schools, dressed in the same uniforms at Port Said School in Cairo, and experienced most of the same educational excursions that our parents took us to. As young adults, we had separate lives, but whenever I went back to Malaysia for visits, I was mostly parked at his home on the island of Langkawi.

Malek used to be a skipper for private boats, a diving instructor and we used to dance together in clubs, and now he's devoted his life to a path that, in my view, is extreme. He neglects the essential teachings of contributing to society and the importance of family, and he disregards his wife when he's off for 40 days during the Tabligh "retreats," contrary to the Prophet's admonishment against neglecting one's family for the sake of prayer.

This is what happens when we don't use our God-given brains, which the Quran repeatedly instructs us to use to contribute to the betterment of society. The religious authorities know this, but instead, they have too many Muslims blindly following them, propagating half-truths, and shaping followers into docile sheep to expand their own flocks, resulting in influence and power. Our parents taught us the basic tenet that we should never relinquish our gifts from God, especially our capacity for critical thinking. It is therefore frustrating to witness my brother succumb to a version of faith that omits the essence of the teachings—to think critically!

***

While in Cairo, we lived in a new neighborhood, Dokki, and this new enclave gifted us a view of the Pyramids from our verandah. That was between the years 1969 and 1974. I am told that this view is probably unlikely now, as everything has been built up, obscuring any view of the Pyramids unless you're right there on its premises.

During one of the many visits to the Pyramids, at the plaza, there are always folks peddling their goods, begging, and persuading you to rent their donkeys or camel rides. As we continued to walk as a family, I usually straggled behind, daydreaming and just taking in life at my pace. As I was lagging behind, I was walking in the direction of a man with two children sitting on a brown cardboard. He saw me walking toward him; he smiled and tore off a piece of *baladi,* a round brown, pita-bread, and extended his arm to offer it to me.

In the era of terrorism and suicide missions, poor people have often been maligned, taking the blame for acts of terrorism. Just because one is poor doesn't mean they are radicalized.

The example of this poor man and his kind smile and generosity in giving a piece of the one bread he had is an example that debunks the notion that poverty equals radicalism. It is the poor who are manipulated by the rich and sophisticated. It isn't the rich who strap themselves with explosives, is it?

The teaching of generosity, of giving is one of the five pillars of Islam and is very ingrained in Muslim cultures. Go to any home in Malaysia, and even your poorest neighbor would invite you in and ask "*sudah makan?*" meaning, have you eaten? And in the reporting we hear back from Western-based doctors who have volunteered in Gaza, there have been ample stories of Palestinians sharing their only hot meal of the day with doctors.

***

In the tapestry of religious discourse, half-truths persist as a pervasive theme, especially within the Muslim world. Unlike its illustrious Golden Era, the Muslim world is entangled in a web of poverty, spiritual deprivation, intellectual stagnation, and financial instability. Learned religious scholars, while well-versed in theology, often withhold essential truths from the masses. What they disseminate in schools and congregations is confined to the realms of permissibility (*halal*) and prohibition (*haram*), the latter category seemingly expanding and growing longer with each passing year. This deliberate expansion of prohibitions mirrors man-made controls aimed at stifling individual thought and expression.

One glaring example of this manipulation lies within Sharia courts, widely and wildly understood as God's law by the

Muslim populace. It isn't. Sharia law is a 100 per cent man-made set of laws. Sharia law became the perfect legal manipulation that religious authorities could use for political gains.

To put it simply: if Sharia law is God's law, then why is it different in different countries?

For instance, the Sharia laws in Afghanistan markedly differ from those in Pakistan, Iran, Saudi Arabia, and Malaysia, showcasing the arbitrary nature of these regulations. I have challenged the divinity of Sharia law plenty of times, even offering a quick lesson when I was on Sean Hannity's show on Fox, and oddly enough, and for different reasons, both ends of the spectrum prefer to believe that Sharia law is divine.

My sister, Zurina, is very rational, intelligent and a graduate of Sharia law from the prestigious 1,000-year-old al-Azhar University. It is the Sunni Islamic learning center, and therefore graduates from this institution are usually highly respected. But not from me. Even as a rational human being, when it comes to matters of Islam, all logical thinking goes out the window. This circles back to the issue of the impermissibility of critical thinking in religious discourse in traditional schools, starting from pre-K and all the way up to al-Azhar University.

Zurina dismisses my argument against the absurdity of Sharia law as God's law as an uneducated analysis, whereas I argue back with an example. In Malaysia, it is amusing to see how Sharia laws have changed over time particularly on matters of polygamy. Years ago, men were required to prove they could provide for their first wife and children before the judge gave men permission to marry wife number two. Men were also required to seek permission from wife number one. That is not the case anymore. So, what happened? God came down and gave this Malaysian Sharia court a new set of laws?

One doesn't have to be a graduate of Sharia law from al-Azhar University to poke a huge hole in that farcity.

Over the years because my sister is a graduate of this prestigious university, everything she says to my family is assumed as truth, pitting me as the sinful one and in need to be "saved." This has resulted in a strained relationship between us and especially between my mother and me. Once Zurina started posting on my Facebook profile page with negative comments about me, I decided to block her. The most liberating aspect about aging is that I have given myself permission to draw the boundaries in my relationships. Unfortunately, though, it took me too long to get to this point. In my Asian culture, we were raised to respect our elders, and therefore we don't draw boundaries, resulting in our elders taking advantage and being abusive.

As a feminist and human rights advocate within the context of Islam, my endeavors have focused on challenging the State's definition of Islam, and on how they justify abhorrent abusive policies in the name of religion. And for many governments, having a critical-thinking Muslim population that can decipher what is truth and what is political is not good for their politics. This advocacy has not come without its challenges. During the tenure of ex-Malaysian Prime Minister Najib Razak, between the years of 2017 to 2018, a group of us Malay progressives and feminists faced relentless attacks by Najib on a daily basis. This ex-Malaysian Prime Minister was quoted to have said "feminist and progressive Muslims are more danger-ous to our society than ISIS." Funded directly from the Prime Minister's office, these campaigns unleashed derogatory arti-cles published on a dedicated website "Menara Malaysia," and swiftly disseminated across social media. Those articles were then shared in large WhatsApp groups, and those individuals in the WhatsApp group would then share them on various other social media platforms, especially Facebook. They had mastered the technique of always having their perspectives go viral.

The vitriol escalated to death threats and slanderous narra-tives, labeling us as apostates deserving of punishment. Vile narratives such as "these Muslims are apostates," or "her blood is *halal*" were common phrases. The term *halal* in this context means, it is permissible to kill an apostate. For some conserv-ative and all radical Muslims, being an apostate means you have abandoned or relinquished Islam and that you deserve to die. Saudi Arabia, Iran, and Afghanistan behead apostates, and in Pakistan, vigilantes will take matters into their own hands and kill "apostates. " Even my efforts to report these threats to social media platforms were met with dismissive responses, exacerbating our vulnerability.

When I wrote to complain to Facebook about the threats and that they needed to take the posts down, many days later I got an email response, expressing they didn't find anything offen-sive and that, "It seems to be a robust conversation"! Hate and death threats never fail to feed into a robust hate fest. Years later we find out Facebook's *laissez faire* attitude toward death threats resulted in the genocide of Rohingyas in Myanmar.

In November 2015, we were organizing a conference to launch *Komunuti Muslim Universal* (KMU), a sister organization of MPV in Kuala Lumpur. The hotel we had booked was threatened by the religious authorities, JAKIM, to reveal the names and contact information of our partners. JAKIM said "If you don't, we will raid the event on the day of, and arrest the Muslims." Copying from Saudi Arabia's radical Wahhabism days, JAKIM are the so-called moral police. When JAKIM raids a public event in the name of religion, they separate the Muslims and the non-Muslims. The non-Muslims are set free, and the Muslims are booked on various charges of "immoral" activities and referred for hearing at the Sharia court. The hotel we had booked for the conference notified us and we had to publicly cancel the event but secretly moved it to a new hotel location all within 48 hours. The launching of the conference with our sister organization proceeded successfully and without a hitch. Participants and diplomats were informed of the new location, and they all understood how important it was to keep the location a secret.

Here's a tip. Having diplomats at the launch was also a deterrent to the Malaysian government and its religious enforcers. They wouldn't want to be caught up in a diplomatic uproar. And we knew that.

With my American passport in hand, I landed at the airport in Malaysia for the launch. The immigration officer said,

"Zuriani, you haven't done any production work here lately."
I was flagged. Given the threats from the religious authorities,
JAKIM, and the online death threats, I was so concerned about
my security that I ended up staying at a friend's residence with
tall gates rather than at the hotel where the conference was
to be held.

Despite these challenges, our response was far from passive.
Our resilience, coupled with the support of progressive individuals and diplomats, allowed us to launch KMU successfully, albeit in secrecy. The experience, though daunting, has
fortified my determination to challenge the status quo and
expose the hypocrisy that often lurks beneath the facade of
religious piety.

Now, I'm a very nice person, but I wasn't going to let them
punch me or our local partners down the way they did with
slander and death threats, and get away with it. So, the
counter-offensive began. We wrote responses in Malay to
their slanderous pieces and posted them as a direct response
on their Facebook profiles. We found out who the "anony-
mous" authors of the articles were; we published posts with
their photos, their faces on them and with a red "x" mark, with
the Arabic word *fitnah*, which means, one who creates social
chaos. We used religious language they used against us on
them, something no one had ever dared to do before.

In an attempt to quell our progressive movement, the
Malaysian administration went so far as to produce a
television series, on Astro cable, *Jalan Sesat Ke Syurga*
which means "The Lost Way to Heaven," depicting a

female imam leading mixed-gender and unsegregated prayer congregation—a practice in line with our progressive beliefs, and it's exactly the manner in which we held prayers at MPV! (Photo: Astro woman imam) For such a religious-themed television show to be created, the writers and producers would have received official instructions from JAKIM, which exemplified the lengths to which they would go to counter our movement. That's proof of how the sociocultural-political-religious system works in Malaysia.

> Nampak ni dekat FB. Macam drama ajaran sesat. Perempuan jadi imam, ade makmum yang tak pakai telekung dan sebaris dengan lelaki.
>
> No more drama melayu yang cliche. "Jalan Sesat Ke Syurga". Akan keluar 3 august di Astro Prima.
> Translate Tweet

3:15 AM · Jul 26, 2020 · Twitter for Android

**13.6K** Retweets and comments   **15.4K** Likes

**Figure 8:** Astro woman imam

Personally, I became the target of relentless smear campaigns. Their epic attack on me culminated with having my face plastered on the cover of a very popular Malay tabloid, "Kosmo!" This was June 20, 2017. The heading in bold "Who is Ani Zonneveld aka Zuriani Tan Sri Datuk Abdul Khalid Awang Osman." In other words, the government's intrusion into my personal life even extended to unearthing my maiden name, further intensifying the assault into family shaming.

The contents of the article condemned my egalitarian views of Islam and included several *muftis* or religious authorities stating that I would go to hell unless I repent. And that's not all. Also on the front cover was a picture of my father and his biography.

It was over a phone conversation with my oldest brother Azahari that I found out about the tabloid and how, according to the family consensus, "I've put the family's name to shame." That didn't go down well with my mother and the conservative members of my family. Azahari, who had been a staunch supporter of me, kept them at bay. After a moment of silence, he said: "Well, thanks to you, the whole of Malaysia finally knows how our father contributed to the country!" To which we both burst out laughing!

Despite my grievances with many religious "leaders," I have been fortunate to partner with many whom I consider to be brave truth-tellers, amidst a sea of falsehoods. "Pure" is how I would describe the best of them. They are usually the most sincere, humble, mindful, kind, smart, and the most truthful. These individuals will walk the straight-and-narrow path of truth rather than compromise their values.

In contemporary spiritual and mindfulness teachings, concepts like "manifesting", and intentionality have gained popularity. Sorry folks, this is nothing new. In Islam, it is all about "intention," and if your intentions are pure, the universe will manifest your intentions. This profound connection to the universe resonates deeply with me, perhaps echoing the animist traditions of my ancestors of centuries ago.

In my quest for spiritual enlightenment, I've often found solace in the rituals of others, particularly the Navajo practice of prayer, which I learned at an interfaith camp for children that my daughter and I attended.

First, you write your prayer or intentions down, wrap it in a cloth, and tie it to a branch of a tree. The winds will blow your prayer and intentions into the universe for it to learn of your intentions and prayers, and for it then to manifest your prayer. I found this moving, the connectivity between our intentions and the universe incredibly beautiful.

Scientifically, Neil deGrasse Tyson's explanation of our biological connection to the stars resonated as the truest description of spirituality: "The atoms of our bodies are traceable to stars that manufactured them in their cores and exploded these enriched ingredients across our galaxy, billions of years ago. For this reason, we are biologically connected to every other living thing in the world."

At a National Geographic Channel launch event of its documentary "The Story of God" featuring Morgan Freeman, deGrasse Tyson was also in attendance, and I had the chance to thank Tyson personally for how he helped my husband understand me better. From the way he looked at me, I could tell he was amused—at how he, an atheist, unintentionally helped my husband understand my Muslim spirituality, showcasing his profound ability of communication.

Yet, amidst these profound spiritual connections, the pettiness of human-made taboos becomes glaringly evident. Some male religious leaders that I encountered in the West shun simple gestures of human connection, refusing handshakes and eye contact due to false interpretations that all intergender touching may lead to illicit and sinful thoughts. It's a bit like Vice President Mike Pence when he claims he would never dine or attend an event where alcohol is served without his wife.

As a human being operating in a spiritual space, the idea of sexual attraction is usually the furthest from my mind. In the Malay tradition that I was raised in, we greeted each other regardless of sex by touching both hands together, and then placing your hands to your heart. It was a gesture to indicate acceptance of the other person's greeting to heart. And if someone is going to be turned on by that, then that's a pathetic human being. The handshake taboo is new, about forty years old, and other recent man-made rules—such as segregated entrances to mosques, classrooms, and socializing starkly contrasts with Islam's history.

If we are supposed to be brothers and sisters, then shaking hands or even hugging each other shouldn't be construed as anything more than a genuine show of affection. With some of the religious leaders that I work with, we hug, because they are my spiritual brothers. These prohibitions, restricting the basic expressions of human affection, strike me as artificial barriers to human connection and our shared humanity.

The issue of hate speech and the slandering of personalities online is something I've experienced, not just from the Malaysian government, but from the Christian and Muslim Right too. After Trump won the first election, I received death threats from strangers emboldened by his hate speech. But there are rules and policies that govern hate speech, and that are clearly defined in "The Istanbul Process." It is a United Nations intergovernmental policy framework for "Combating intolerance, negative stereotyping and stigmatization of, and discrimination, incitement to violence and violence against, persons based on religion or belief." This definition has been agreed to by member states, or governments, including ours. The fact that this is clearly spelled out is designed to protect people like you and me, and especially those that late Congressman John Lewis described as "good trouble," in the framework that allows us to hold governments and those attacking us accountable.

If you think the problem of scrupulous governments is just "there," it has come to roost in the US. In 2024, Congress passed two bills that are problematic. H.R. 6408 and H.R. 9495—that will allow for the Secretary of the Treasury to unilaterally strip a 501 (c)(3) nonprofit organization of its status for "supporting terrorism," without having to show evidence for it. It should be noted that it is already illegal for any American entity to support terrorism anyway. This bill was crafted in November 2023, and at the heart of this bill is the effort by Zionist organizations and some legislatures to silence pro-Palestinian protestors made up of a broad coalition of Muslims, Jews, Christians, Indigenous and Black organizations, as well as nonprofit media outlets like The Intercept. However, because of the bill's broad language, if it becomes law, it will strip any nonprofit organizations—such as civil societies, media, charities, and religious institutions challenging the American government on any of its policies, can be labeled as supporting terrorism. This bill, nicknamed "Non-Profit Killer Bill" conflicts with our constitutional rights. It has the chilling effect of stifling dissent, freedom of speech, and freedom of assembly, which are the foundations of a democracy.

Of course, since the election of President Trump, he has governed by threatening institutions. If you care about democracy, then you should pay close attention to how it is being unraveled, and fight back like hell.

The United Nations Declaration of Human Rights is a document of ideals, and then there's reality. The language of hate is constantly debated, and it was a topic of discussion for a panel that I was on at an Istanbul Process conference titled "No Tolerance for Intolerance" at The Hague in 2019. Generally speaking, because of the European legacy of the Holocaust and their history of murderous colonial excursions, Western policymakers are very sensitive to intolerance and hate speech directed across race, ethnicity, and religion by one group toward another. There are exceptions of course. For some segments of European society demonization of the LGBT+ community is just below the surface, whereas that toward Muslims is above the surface, and with some governments, it is an outright hate fest—with plenty of allies here in the US.

Navigating this complex landscape of politics and religion has made me clear-eyed on the intricacies of discrimination within religious communities or the manner in which politicians utilize hate of the other. For many decades Muslims and immigrants in the West have been on the receiving end of this campaign, especially during election season. The normalization of this hate manifested itself as in the rampage described in Chapter 5 in response to the killing of five young British girls of a Taylor Swift dance club. It is worth repeating: Muslims were falsely accused, and their businesses and mosques were attacked and, in some instances, burned down in the UK in August 2024.

This is a good indicator of the level of hate from a segment of the general public toward Muslims and immigrants. And this is not a good indicator.

At the heart of any genocide is hate speech, and we humans have a fantastic record for inflicting violence on a massive scale. Just before the Holocaust there was the Armenian genocide, and since then there was the Cambodian genocide where, in 1975, about two million people were killed by the Khmer Rouge. There's the Srebrenica massacre where the Serbs attempted to extinct 40,000 Bosnian Muslims; the slaughter of almost 900,000 Tutsi by the Hutus in the span of three days; the slaughter of Rohingya Muslims by the Buddhist regime of Myanmar, there's the Yazidi genocide by the terrorist group ISIS, and the latest is the genocide of Palestinians by Israel.

On the international fora, I see many Western democracies championing against hate speech because of this genocidal history of human beings, but there are exceptions.

Despite the hateful political language of the Israeli government, voted in by the members of its society in a democratic process, and the "live" broadcast of the extermination of Palestinians, Western governments have refused to act upon their legal mandate as a result of signing on to the Convention on the Prevention and Punishment of the Crime of Genocide. The Convention stipulates the definition of a genocide, the responsibility to prevent one, and the legal responsibility of governments to prosecute perpetrators. But instead, we have seen America and some of the European governments renege on their responsibility "to prevent" a genocide, and have instead continued to support in every which way, including arming Israel with 2,000 pound bombs. In a nutshell, these governments are complicit, the biggest culprit of all is the American government under the Biden administration, and with Trump fantasizing of a Trump Tower in Gaza.

Western democracies that have championed international human rights laws, and numerous international conventions have shown their hypocritical human rights standards. It simply doesn't apply to Palestinians. The general public, especially young Jews who have woken up to the ethnic cleansing process in the creation of Israel, are angry. I completely understand that anger. It is anger at the betrayal of our human values and rage by "how dare you do these atrocities in my name." I felt the same rage at the perpetrators of 9/11 and ISIS.

The difference is, these are terrorist entities and not democratically voted in by me or any Muslim, while the Israeli government is.

For the 2023 Christmas sermon, "Liturgy of Lament: Christ in the Rubble" (Isaac, 2023), the Palestinian Evangelical pastor, Dr Reverend Munther Isaac, said it best: "I never want to hear you (Western democracies) lecture us on human rights and international law again!"

Now there's a truth-teller.

\*\*\*

# 8
# Solving the problem of women and girls' rights

One of the countries I have worked in for the past nine years is Burundi, where I've witnessed firsthand the transformative power of community-led initiatives. Just as my great-grandfather was an influencer in his community, it has been a strange coincidence—but a comfortable one—for me to now be working with village imams, influencers in their own right.

Inspired by UN Women's #HeForShe campaign, we developed the #ImamsForShe program in which imams are trained in how to preach, engage, and champion for women's and girls' rights, and relate them to their lived experiences. Infused in the three-day workshop is a short theater skit to help reinforce the values with an emotional memory that will propel their activism. Once the imams have completed their training, they are obligated to preach these egalitarian values for their Friday sermons.

Now, in our ninth year of implementing #ImamsForShe, we've built a network of 3,400 imams and community leaders, working together and in support of each other as they work against the radical tide across Burundi, the Democratic Republic of the Congo, and Rwanda, united in the pursuit of truth and equality.

Why did I start in Burundi? Mostly because a brave young imam, Khalfan Burkuru Ellie, wanted to see change in his community. He was fed up with seeing young girls married off, domestic violence, women deprived of their basic rights to self-determination, to economic independence, and the radicalization of the Muslim society. His heart was drawn to the true teachings of the Quran, and he wanted to practice the real thing.

In analyzing some of the underlying issues, we asked some hard questions. What is at the root of poverty in Muslim societies? In comparison to co-nationalists of a different religion, why are Muslim women and girls absent or disproportionately lower in higher educational institutions? Why is it hard to find qualified and experienced women to hire? Why is domestic violence rampant?

At the root of these seemingly agnostic issues is the false preaching of religious leaders who promote the idea that a woman's place is at home, that wife-beating is permissible, and that girls should be married off as soon as they reach puberty so therefore "there is no point educating them." Sadly, this twisted narrative is the norm in many Muslim societies, propagating this patriarchal regressive interpretation.

In this Muslim-minority country, where the percentage of young Muslim women in universities is alarmingly low compared to their Christian counterparts, Muslims are marginalized, mostly self-segregated in rural areas in the north. There are two reasons for this: one is colonial history, and the second is the domination of misogynistic and hateful preaching by radical imams.

Radical imams often advocate for the segregation of Muslims from the wider society, fostering harmful narratives about non-Muslims, and promoting radical, supremacist ideologies among the youth with their interpretation of Islam as being the only legitimate one and silencing all other schools of thought. These sheikhs are only out for themselves; they prioritize their own agendas over the well-being of society or that of their own nation, operating as well-funded entities dedicated to spreading hate and violence.

From the research we conducted, radical imams in Burundi, the Democratic Republic of the Congo, and Rwanda are mostly groomed in the Gulf States. The prime candidates are Muslim men who barely made it through elementary school, plucked out of their dim prospects for a fully funded university education in Islamic studies from the likes of the University of Medina in Saudi Arabia. Upon graduation, they return home with the religious title "Sheikh" and with lots of cash. They get paid a monthly stipend of USD 5,000, a new car, and a bungalow, and, of course, funds to start a new mosque or *madrassa*.

Not only are we up against the well-funded radical imams, we're also swimming against the historical experiences of a once-colonized Burundi. In Chapter 4, I wrote about how the only school system there was, run by Belgium's Catholic

Church and that, in order to gain admission, students were forced to change their name to a Christian one. Many Muslims refused to do so, and that, in a nutshell, is the back-story for why today there is a lower percentage of educated Muslims.

This history of defiance against the colonizers also contributed to a legacy of self-segregation which has resulted in limited educational opportunities and increased poverty rates among Muslims. Despite this historical legacy, my partners in Burundi and I have worked hard toward dismantling these historical barriers by creating a culture in which you can be Muslim without self-segregating yourself from the rest of society. When Muslims integrate, it also diminishes the fear that non-Muslims may harbor toward their Muslim counterparts, promoting harmony and cohesion among all citizens.

One significant chapter of my work in Burundi was when I met the former Grand Mufti of Burundi, Sheikh Abdallah Sadiki Kajandi. Grand muftis are the highest-ranking religious authority in the country. In the case of Burundi, they are usually elected by their community members as their representative to the government. In addition, some grand Muftis are also handpicked as adviser to the country's president on matters of Islam and its Muslim population. Sheikh Kajandi's endorsement of our #ImamsForShe program was therefore pivotal, providing us cover and support in challenging the norms within his own Muslim communities.

In 2019, I made my second visit to Burundi. As I was boarding the plane and making my way to the economy class, I noticed an Arab man sitting in business class dressed in his traditional robe, *thawb*. I thought to myself, why would an Arab man go to Burundi, a very poor country? When we disembarked and entered the immigration hall, I saw Sheikh Kajandi chatting with the man. Upon seeing me, the sheikh, a well-known figure in his country, came over and greeted me with a brotherly hug. Needless to say, many jaws dropped, including that of the Arab man. As I was getting my visa processed, I could hear my name, "American, Malaysia," in an animated conversation between the two men in Arabic. Inside, I was giggling.

Later I found out that this Arab man visits Burundi every other month, and is the paymaster of the radical imams.

Sheikh Kajandi recognized the importance and value in what we are doing, that is, holding religious leaders accountable for their preaching. This sentiment was also expressed to me in clear terms with a firm handshake from the Grand Mufti of Uganda, Dr Sheikh Shaban Ramadhan Mubaje, in 2022.

Kajandi's support for our work by officiating and speaking at our events and workshops, and his attendance at a remote village with us at our #ClubsForShe camp for young women was instrumental in our success (Photo: ClubsForShe). He helped the parents and the young women trust our initiative and our imams. The grand mufti's willingness to stand with us against prevailing falsehoods demonstrated the power of pure intentions, truth and solidarity.

**Figure 9:** ClubsForShe

Kajandi passed away on March 11, 2024. I will forever be in debt for his brotherly love, his bravery to show it, and his commitment to truth.

*** 

My first trip to Bujumbura, Burundi, was in 2018, to observe the implementation of our programs. As a side event, I was invited to speak to a group of 75 mothers about child marriages at one of our partnering mosques. The mothers, and some with babies, sat on a mat on the ground while the imams, the translator Aminah, and I were sitting on a chair. In his introduction of me, the imam made sure to inform the audience that I am a Muslim, even though I was not wearing a headscarf, and "that there are many ways to be a Muslim." He continued his introduction by stating that I was a Malaysian residing in the

United States and "who is a dear friend of our community, who has been supporting our programming." This introduction was necessary in setting the stage of acceptance for what I was about to speak about.

The task was daunting: convincing these mothers, deeply rooted in tradition, to encourage their daughters to pursue education and to shun early marriages. I approached this challenge rooted in Islamic principles. Marriage, I emphasized, is a contract between consenting adults. A child cannot negotiate such a contract due to their immaturity. Additionally, Islamic dowries, or *mehr*, are meant for the bride, not the parents, a fact that is often overlooked.

"Many of you take that *mehr* for yourselves, and that is *haram*, forbidden." Some mothers smiled sheepishly, some nodded solemnly. "Thirdly, how much is the *mehr*, $300, $500? That is nothing. If your daughter is educated, she can get a job and support you for life! Isn't that better than $300?" To which they all smiled broadly.

By illustrating the financial benefits of education over a meager dowry, I managed to break through with the mothers by framing this as religiously and financially beneficial for their daughters, the mothers themselves and their families.

Communities prosper when women are educated and financially empowered. In our years of work in Burundi, we witnessed a profound change: mosques became hubs of egalitarian ideals, with our imams gaining trust and popularity, marked by well-attended congregational prayers, more girls attending higher education, and the womenfolk starting up businesses. The simple truth is that when religious leaders uplift women's and girls' rights, everyone benefits. It's a win-win-win for everyone.

The formula is simple: the community becomes what you teach. If hate is promoted, then we breed a society marred by hatred. This is evident not only within Muslim communities but also across various faiths and cultures. We see extremism inspired by hate-preaching in the Christian Right in America, radical Judaism in Israel and America, the Buddhist monks in Myanmar, and the Hindutva movement in India. Hate speech is not exclusive to the religious domain but has flourished in political speeches, and has escalated with each election cycle in America.

*** 

Unlike our #ImamsForShe, when religious leaders are morally corrupt, exploitation of women and girls perpetuates a cycle of suffering that is evident in the deprivation of education, and so many other rights like in Afghanistan, and let's not forget Malala who got shot in the face for promoting schooling for girls in Pakistan.

Temporary marriages, also known as *sigheh* or *misyar*, involve an arrangement where there is no long-term commitment or financial obligation from the man to the woman, even in the event of pregnancy. For traditionalists, illicit sex is forbidden, all forms of extramarital relations are prohibited, and some will therefore resort to temporary marriages officiated by a religious leader in the name of God. This loophole allows them to engage in guilt-free sexual relationships.

In Indonesia, temporary marriages are essentially sex tourism, with clientele primarily from the Gulf States. In the Syrian refugee camps in Jordan, due to poverty, young girls are married off to richer suitors primarily from the Gulf. The imam officiating these marriages is compensated and is morally corrupt, for marriage is supposed to be between two consenting adults. The parents keep the *mehr*, and the groom fulfills his sexual desires.

To put it harshly, this is not much different than pimping your child. More often than not, after a few months shacked up in an apartment, the rich husband abandons the young woman and returns to his home country. In conservative communities, losing your virginity and being divorced at a young age is seen as a disgrace.

Temporary marriages are also rampant in Iraq, and they are not much different than a religiously sanctioned form of prostitution. In this practice, the imam facilitates these unions, receiving compensation for the marriage services rendered, the bride gets her *mehr,* and the groom fulfills his sexual desires. This is also a win-win-win formula, but even though this arrangement might seem like a mutually beneficial solution, it raises ethical concerns and has negative consequences for society at large.

As a provider of officiant services, in the U.S., where religious marriage holds no legal weight or legitimacy, MPV sometimes receives requests for temporary marriages from young couples, some even seeking polygamous unions, both of which we firmly decline to officiate. College campuses, in particular, become a melting pot of newfound freedoms for young adults away from home, leading to increased social interactions with the opposite sex and the blossoming of romantic relationships. For children raised in strict traditional homes with segregated gender spaces, it is hard to adjust to this overnight freedom to mingle.

Reflecting on my own experiences during my first semester in college in the US, I was struck by the transformation of girls from rural Illinois in my dorm. Many were exploring their newfound freedom and were losing their virginity, and some were living quite promiscuously. As a mature woman, I can empathize with the sense of liberation that young Muslims are experiencing in such environments, but it would have been wiser for Muslim parents to raise their child with freedoms and with the skills to make decisions responsibly.

Even though I work toward ending child and forced marriages in the Global South, it is disheartening to note that in America, child marriage remains a distressing reality. Shockingly, in 2024 and in 37 states, marriage is legally permissible at the age of 16 with parental consent. California, for instance, has seen approximately 20,000 young women under 18 entering marital unions, most are marrying adult men. Many of these girls come from conservative, insular families of various religious backgrounds and are forced into marriage due to diverse reasons, such as unplanned pregnancies, marriages to their own rapists, coercive situations, or attempts to suppress their sexual orientations, whether it be their bisexuality or lesbianism. This sounds like a description of some conservative Muslim country, but no, it's California.

It has been incredibly hard to persuade state legislators to establish a universal marriage age of 18 without exceptions. For some reason, American Civil Liberties Union (ACLU) and Planned Parenthood, our allies on matters such as reproductive justice and LGBTQ+ rights, think it is better for a child to marry than to be in an abusive familial setting.

The American government and private foundations demonstrate considerable dedication and resources in fighting against child and forced marriages in the Global South. Occasionally, our detractors question us with, "Why don't you Americans focus on resolving these issues in your own country first?"

Religion, and in this case Islam, has been exploited in various inappropriate ways. One such instance is the abhorrent practice of Female Genital Mutilation and Cutting (FGM/C). Recognized as torture by the United Nations, this practice has no foundation in Islam, as theologically argued against in *The Golden Book*, yet it continues to be justified in the name of religion.

On a quiet day in December in 2021, I found myself thinking about FGM/C and why it was so hard to eradicate such a violent and harmful practice. The use of religious language to counter religious justification for FGM/C has had limited success. Laws making the practice illegal are flouted. Convincing cutters with alternative vocation has not been fully invested. All these approaches are band-aids but do not address the "why." Women were still the main champions of the practice in their reasoning for pleasing the husband, and the viability of a young woman for marriage if she is cut. So, if women were doing it for men, I thought, how about fighting it at its source, by eliminating the real reason for cutting? Why weren't we asking the men this question: "Is it more sexually fulfilling to have intercourse with a woman who has been cut or one who hasn't?"

With the help of two friends in Kenya and a small stipend, I asked them to interview men about their sexual experiences. Although this was not a broad scientific survey, with the help of government health workers, they managed to gain the trust of the men and women before conducting interviews with various tribes, including the Maasai and Kenyans of Somali heritage. The conclusion was, of course, men preferred sexual intercourse with an uncut woman. One man said: "It is heart-breaking for me to see the pain on my woman's face while I'm penetrating her. It is not pleasant."

I think promoting men's desire to have an uncut woman as a wife can end the practice of FGM/C tomorrow. It is an idea that has never been given a chance.

Publicizing audio files of our interviews with men, and creating social media campaigns in different languages could advance this narrative and would be another tool in the box for eradicating this practice, but traditional feminists balk at this idea, and funders keep funding the same narrative, which after so many decades has not completely worked. It's like a whack-a-mole game.

Women who have undergone FGM/C often experience intense pain during penetration, creating an unpleasant experience for both partners involved. Men who were intimate with cut women struggled to enjoy sexual pleasures while inflicting pain on their lover or wife. Additionally, the diminished sexual satisfaction of women significantly affects men's own experiences where the potential for shared pleasure is limited or absent.

We also found that Muslim Kenyans of Somali heritage and with the financial means, tended to have their first wife from Somali heritage and cut, adhering to their cultural traditions, while the second wife would be from the coastal cities such as Mombasa, where Muslim Kenyan women were not cut.

Furthermore, conversations with women who had undergone FGM revealed that unsatisfactory sexual relationships between spouses had wider repercussions within the family. This dissatisfaction and frustration often led to domestic violence, which tragically affected the children. It all boiled down to FGM/C being the cause for an unhealthy and unhappy family dynamic.

It is perplexing how the cycle of such a destructive and harmful practice keeps perpetuating itself with no winners, apart from the cutters who profit financially from these procedures.

In the case of the Maasai tribe, having a cut wife contributes significantly to their social and economic structure. Husbands with cut wives are granted membership in the village leadership council, while the wives become part of the group responsible for crafting souvenirs sold to tourists, a vital source of income for their community. Having visited a Maasai village in Kenya, the pressure to buy souvenirs is intense.

This perpetuates the cycle, intertwining harmful traditions with social and economic incentives, creating a complex web that continues to impact generations. This web needs to be undone.

Advocates and organizations tend to work in silos in our respective fields of expertise, and there isn't enough collaboration horizontally. For example, there are organizations that work on advancing anti-FGM/C laws, but don't do the work of changing the culture in the community to support the laws. Culture is influenced by religion, and we therefore need to counter the practice in religious language, but most funders don't fund faith based advocacy. Laws can change, and as we have seen in The Gambia in 2024, the criminalization of FGM/C was almost decriminalized because the culture against FGM/C had not yet baked in. There were still too many people, religious leaders and legislators who wanted to go back to an old harmful tradition. In Kenya, FGM has been illegal since 2011 but it has now gone underground. Girls are cut at private clinics, and the new term for that is medicalized cutting.

Another way to look at this is, we have laws against stealing, but people still do!

In addition to the tools already utilized toward eradicating FGM/C—laws, religion, vocational training of cutters with an alternative skill, we must dispel the myth that men prefer cut women. This must be part of the intersectional strategies cross-training each other in our specific expertise.

***

Given my upbringing as the child of an ambassador, I am comfortable sitting at the table with diplomats and policymakers, as comfortable as I am working with the religious leaders that I partner with. I can talk in their respective languages, but I do believe above all that the language that cuts through is honesty. People can feel it.

In advance of making my first trip to Geneva in 2014 to host a panel titled "Islamic Human Rights" at a side event at the Human Rights Council, I sent off cold emails to various ambassadors and secretaries of Permanent Missions introducing our initiative #ImamsForShe. Permanent Missions are equivalent to embassies with an ambassador representing their government at the United Nations. To my surprise, the ambassador of the Dutch Mission at that time, Roderick Van Schreven, and the Chief at the Middle East and North Africa (MENA) desk at the Human Rights Commissioner's office wrote back.

Representing the MENA region was the Swiss-Tunisian Frej Fenniche, who, upon learning about MPV's #ImamsForShe initiative, introduced me to his network of contacts built over decades of human rights work, including progressive Muslim human rights experts and theologians. One such person was Yadh Ben Achour, who also sat on the Human Rights Committee at the UN office in Geneva. As a side note, Yadh also happens to be the grandson of an iconic Tunisian theologian, Sheikh Tahar Ibn Achour, whose writings I utilize in our advocacy work! So as you can probably imagine, I was quite starstruck by all the brains around me!

At the UN there are various legal mechanisms in which Member States (countries) are reviewed in accordance with the UN Declaration of Human Rights and many other treaties, a few of which I've already explained earlier.

There's one story worth sharing is the review of Pakistan at the Human Rights Committee. Pakistan is infamous for its apostasy and blasphemy laws. It claims to be Islamic but the laws are applied in a manner that defies justice. MPV has filed several country reports on the abuse of apostasy and blasphemy laws of Muslim-majority countries challenging their religious basis when it is actually a political tool to silence critical thinking and dissent. These few sentences about the apostasy and blasphemy laws work that we do require a chapter unto themselves, but this will suffice for now.

As a member of the Committee and being an Islamic scholar, Yadh asked the Pakistani government representative point-blank, "Where in the Quran does it state death for apostates?"

The diplomat was dumbstruck and replied, "I will have to check with headquarters." Such a challenge, on a religious basis, was never made prior to this session which was streamed on UN TV. Because the UN is a secular institution, folks are not knowledgeable enough or are too scared to touch on religion. Again, it is important to have allies working with you in their various capacities, sharing the same goals, but with a different set of tools.

Having been an ambassador in Syria before the Arab Uprising, Roderick right away understood the relevance of #ImamsForShe and ended up becoming a true champion of the initiative. While at the helm of the Netherlands Permanent Mission in Geneva, he and his wife hosted a private lunch at his residence introducing me and the work we do to 12 other ambassadors. And to unwind after the successful luncheon, his Secretary of Human Rights, Paul Peters, and I had a game of table tennis! Paul beat me by the way, and I have not had the opportunity for a redo.

Over four years, the Dutch Mission and MPV developed a tradition in which we co-organized and co-chaired events promoting #ImamsForShe. We flew in #ImamsForShe partners from Burundi, Tunisia, and the UK to conduct a workshop for fellow human rights defenders and diplomats. And before he left his post, he introduced me to the new ambassador, ensuring we continued the tradition until COVID forced the world to its knees.

Educating diplomats is also an aspect of my work, it gives them an insight into a very different approach to upholding human rights, knowledge that they report back to their foreign ministries. This then opens the door for me to work directly with their foreign ministry, which enables me to connect their embassies with our local partners in the field that are doing excellent work but are invisible. Embassies also sometimes need to be introduced to small and community-based organizations that don't have the political strings or understand the role of a local foreign embassy, especially ones that provide funding. That's where I come in. I help open doors for the organizations I trust.

\*\*\*

Empowering human rights efforts by leveraging the human psychology of self-interest can be highly effective, a winning formula, except in the presence of entrenched, powerful patriarchal structures resistant to change. To challenge these structures, it is best to bypass them by empowering women through education, specifically emphasizing their right to self-determination. Through our extensive network of religious leaders in Burundi, DRC, and Rwanda, we organize overnight leadership camps called #ClubsForShe. We also incorporate and implement critical-thinking exercises for young women ages 18–25. These sessions delve into topics such as the harms of early marriages and female genital mutilation/cutting (FGM/C). We also focus on educating young women about their rights in Islam and under international human rights treaties such as the Commission on the Status of Women (CEDAW). The discussions encompass their rights to work outside their homes, to earn a living, and to manage their own finances; their right to decide when, if, and whom they marry; assert their rights in marriage; and educate them about options in family planning. Through all these initiatives, we liberate them from chokeholds that suffocate women's and girls' aspirations.

I remember witnessing one of these critical thinking exercises in person, which had me floored. The imam training the 35 young women started playing the "telephone game," which is the game in which an original phrase is whispered to person #1, and that person whispers the phrase to person #2, and so on and so forth. The last person, #35 stated the phrase she heard out loud. The imam then asked person #1 to say the phrase she heard from the imam out loud. Everyone burst into laughter at how twisted the original phrase had become. To that point, the imam said, "In the few minutes we played this game, you can see how distorted the original phrase became. Now just imagine the *hadith*, sayings of Prophet Muhammad attributed to him 200 years after he died! When you hear a *hadith* that sounds ridiculous, make sure to think critically about it, research it first."

This was the critical-thinking exercise they did in a rural village in Burundi. Meanwhile, in the modern and progressive city of Los Angeles, based on the experience my daughter went through, children were taught to be "sheeps."

One of my favorite parts of the #ClubsForShe program is to teaching volunteerism and a sports activity, to teach young Muslim women prohibited from playing sports the liberating feeling of simply running. One of the best memories of my work was playing soccer in one of the most rural areas of Burundi. The team was made up of young women in our #ClubsForShe workshop playing against the village boys. The referee was a city official, and the imams conducting the workshop were the linesmen, with banana leaves as the flags.

Upon completion of the program, each young woman received a certificate. Just as the network of #ImamsForShe is a supportive system for like-minded religious leaders, the graduates of this leadership camp #ClubsForShe established a network of cohorts that would support each other as they stepped out to challenge the patriarchal status quo. What is most important is that the young women in #ClubsForShe will always have the backing of the #ImamsForShe Champions to protect them from any backlash from their new self-empowering outlook.

Incrementally changing attitudes about women's and girls' rights, allowed for new ideas to take root before building on them. This process requires patience to effect sustainable change. To create the ecosystem that allowed for a cultural change, we added on a 30-minute weekly radio program titled "Women's Rights in Islam," hosted by our Imams magnifying the problems in the community and addressing the roots of the problem and how to resolve them.

This public education effort opened up a new way of thinking, it unshackled the community from oppressive and misogynistic teachings. Once women, and especially the public, understood the women's right to work outside the home, that they had the right to do so in Islam, and the right to be economically independent of their husband, we knew we had created a conducive ecosystem that would support women's businesses. The next step was to support them in fulfilling their new aspirations.

In partnership with another organization that provided the seed funding, we created co-ops made up of ten women to start businesses such as opening a store, raising livestock, and farming. Although I am describing this ever so briefly, I want to point out that there were a lot of challenges in starting up businesses for these women, as many of them barely knew how to write or do mathematics. This basic education, as well as management skills, also needed to be taught.

A success story I want to share is the case of a village in Mutaho, in the province of Gitega in Burundi, where a cohort of women started with one store selling sundry and essential household items, and then expanded to five stores. They were so flushed with profit that they made a generous gesture by purchasing and distributing health care cards to village members, regardless of religion or tribe. These health care cards pay 20 per cent of the fees required for a visit to medical facilities; 80 per cent is covered by the government. The positive result, which has been very well documented across multiple disciplines, is that when women do well financially, they build up their families and communities. But remember, this could not have happened without the empowerment of the women themselves and, in this case, with our imams championing the cause for women's rights.

Witnessing the success of others ignited a collective desire for positive change. I have seen this every day when people see others succeed, they, too, want to implement the same changes. Through active involvement with the community, our imams, who are influencers in their own right, and due to their trustworthy reputation, play a pivotal role in unshackling over a hundred years of mental prison and inferiority complexes. This process is essential to liberate minds, elevate the entire village, and become a fundamental part of the progressive values we implement.

Besides educating diplomats and policymakers, I also focus on educating children, as they are the future. Building onto the ecosystem we created where misogynistic religious beliefs were "not cool," I co-designed the development of an Inclusive

Islam Curriculum for Children that centers human rights values in Islamic terms promoting women's and girls' rights, the respect and dignity of all people, and the environment. It is now taught in 68 *madrassas* in Burundi through our network of imams, reaching 10,000 children per year.

In developing the curriculum, I took the United Nations' Sustainable Development Goals (SDGs) and matched them with supporting Quranic verses and *hadiths*. With this foundation, I passed it on to my partner, Imam Khalfan, and his team to create the lesson plans, with comics and dialogue around the issues, followed by critical-thinking exercises and poetry to reinforce those values and the goals. Once the curriculum was developed, we had it endorsed by the late Grand Mufti Cheikh Sadiki Kajàndi Abdallah.

Many Muslim schools or *madrassas* use physical punishment for minor mistakes, like when an Arabic word is mispronounced. Some of these teachers should not be in the teaching profession and are simply child-abusers. The inhumane treatment of children can lead to the development of traumatized and insecure adults, which manifests into various forms of violence, including domestic abuse or radicalization. Violence begets violence, and that is evident in many Muslim societies, where violence against another human being seems to be a low threshold to cross. It is therefore important to break the cycle of violence, starting with schools.

Parents of the children in our program are appreciative that there are nonviolent and alternative methods of teaching children, and one that involves critical thinking around values rather than blind memorization and recitation of the Quran. And the imams, they have been eager to finally have such a curriculum to teach children about women's and girls' rights, respect for others, human dignity, and the environment.

It's a win-win-win for everyone, and for a brighter future.

I believe that to break the cycles of violence, it is essential for Muslim societies, religious authorities, and governments to ban violent teaching methods. Instead, there should be an emphasis on preaching and teaching a loving and compassionate theology. By adopting these principles, within a single generation, I know we will see a positive change in society. This transformation will lead to a more peaceful approach to conflict resolution, creating an environment conducive for a society to flourish and develop.

As an indicator of our success, over time, we started seeing more and more people attending the mosques of our imams from neighboring villages. The local village mosque could usually accommodate 80 to 100 people, and now the spaces were getting overcrowded. The villagers liked our egalitarian messages, and the parents liked our child-centric, nonviolent method of teaching Islam in our *madrassas*. With success comes challenges.

Another indicator of our success is the increase in threats against our imams from radical imams. The question I always ask is, who the hell is paying for radicalism? One important lesson I learned from an old friend with regard to American politics is, "Ani, follow the money, and you will find the answer."

I think this advice, unfortunately, applies to everything in life. As a side note, during election season in America with the plethora of advertisements, I always look at the small print for who are the funders and sponsors of such an advertisement or campaign. Try it. You'll avoid being duped into voting for a wolf in sheep's clothing.

Mahatma Gandhi aptly stated, "First they ignore you, then they laugh at you, then they fight you, then you win." This resonated when threats against our imams increased, signifying our impact on regressive forces.

In the case of Imam Khalfan, my #ImamsForShe partner of nine years, he was randomly arrested and thrown in jail supposedly for "promoting homosexuality." This accusation and arrest came immediately after answering a query from a close confidant about Islam's position on homosexuality, to which the imam responded that there's no punishment for being a homosexual in Islam. On Christmas Day of 2019, I got a call from him sounding very weak. He said he was in jail for four days, all his cellmates were dead, but he was let go. With the help of a doctor friend, he had his blood tested, and they thought it was arsenic poisoning. The prison guards poisoned all the meals and water to ensure whoever they wanted to kill was killed, and the rest would be collateral damage. Besides the agony of being poisoned, the heartbreak from a betrayal by a close confidant was equally agonizing.

Immediately and for weeks, I desperately tried to raise the funds to fly him and his wife out of the country for medical treatment. Through a Dutch diplomat friend, Esther Loefren, we were referred to an organization Defending the Human

Rights Defenders, which covered all the travel and medical expenses as well as the coordination efforts, resources that MPV just doesn't have. Initially, the plan was to fly him out to Uganda, but then our contacts in Uganda were warned that an election was imminent, and the authorities were going to shut down the borders and internet connection. We had to therefore find another safe country, and fortunately, we were able to seek two weeks of treatment in Nairobi. Once well enough, Imam Khalfan was ready to go back to his home country and to "fight even harder for the true teachings of Islam." With enough medication for a month, the imam and his wife returned.

Even though this description of flying him out of one country and into another for treatment seems effortless, it wasn't. When you are from a poor country seeking health care, the "receiving hospital" needs to verify that there are financial funds available before providing the medical care. In this case, Defending the Human Rights Defender was the guarantor. This is just one of my experiences, but imagine so many others who risk their lives daily to lift up their society, and sometimes die doing so.

This story of poisoning is just one example. There were other examples of gunshots fired into his home, or a truck trying to run his car off the winding and hilly roads in rural areas of Burundi.

As I work on human rights issues, I usually work in areas that are radical and dangerous. I venture into regional areas of Tunisia that even the UN would not give security clearance for its officers. In southern DRC, Pope Francis in 2022 was

advised against going to Goma, where the violence is so brutal and gangsterism reigns, but that is where we implement
our #ImamsForShe and #ClubsForShe programs. On a trip to
Burundi, we had a military escort in the car with us at all times,
with his loyal AK-47 gun by his side (Photo: Gun escort).

**Figure 10:** Gun escort

Despite the hurdles, our approach, rooted in love, compassion, and community engagement, has created tangible change. When people are lifted up, it becomes contagious. By dismantling barriers of self-segregation and fostering trust between communities, we've bridged gaps and lessened fear. In one remarkable instance, our imam in Burundi won a parliamentary seat with a staggering 72 per cent majority, proving that genuine care for the community pays off. Through education, economic empowerment, and compassion, we're not just challenging norms; we're reshaping lives, one community at a time, paving the way for a brighter, more inclusive future.

The success of our project took more than three years to come to fruition, a time span that most funders see as their limit. Wallace Global Fund has been the exception, funding in small amounts but consistently for nine years. The success of our #ImamsForShe programs has resulted in them becoming case studies for policy papers and government-funded research.

Publicizing our successes, finding the funds to do this work to support the brave souls who dare to speak the truth within their communities, dismantling the lies woven into the fabric of their societies, and illuminating the path toward a brighter, more equitable future is the least this privileged woman can do.

\*\*\*

# 9
# Becoming an American

According to the Merriam-Webster dictionary, culture encapsulates "the customary beliefs, social forms, and material traits of a racial, religious, or social group," as well as "the characteristic features of everyday existence (such as diversions or a way of life) shared by people in a place or time."

Many years ago, during my college days, I found myself at the Student Union building to get a snack. On one occasion in the public lounge, I came across an animated crowd of baseball enthusiasts engrossed in a game.

I asked, "What are you watching?"

"The World Series" was the response.

Intrigued, I asked, "Which countries are playing?" After all, if it's a "world series" it must be something international related, right? I don't remember what year or what the names of the teams were, but I do remember they were both American teams. The term "World Series" struck me then, as it does now, as a testament to the American psyche, positioning itself as the center of the globe. As someone who was raised to be tuned-in to the cultures of others, I found this self-centered outlook jarring.

In another uniquely American tradition, I was told on several occasions that it is not advisable to discuss money, religion and politics. My first thoughts were, "what a strange culture!" What can you talk about? Since my favorite subjects were off-limits, for a long time I usually didn't start a conversation because I felt the parameters were too narrow, and subsequent conversations shallow.

In my formative years, from the ages of 12 to 16, we lived in New Delhi. I found my passion in soccer at The British School. This private school was like a mini-United Nations. The students were a melting pot of children of diplomats, executives from foreign corporations, United Nations representatives, political refugees, and dissidents. Here, amidst this eclectic mix, I received a firsthand education in world politics, such as the devastating South African apartheid. I learned from my friends who had lived through the politics and its repercussions. Their learning experiences were not just cerebral but personal and therefore emotional.

Zimpande Msimang, whom I am still friends with, and whose father was responsible for setting up the African National Congress (ANC) offices all over the world, was one of my closest friends in school. The ANC offices were the equivalent of an embassy, and as their leader Nelson Mandela was in jail, the establishment of embassies was their way of mobilizing international support for their cause. The ANC's mission was to do away with apartheid and called for "one man, one woman, one vote" for all South Africans. It was incredibly surprising for me at this age to learn that the support against apartheid was from the Communist and the nonaligned countries, and not from Western democracies.

An unexpected beacon from an American entity that did support the divestment of South Africa and the anti-apartheid movement is the iconic Episcopalian Church, All Saints in Pasadena, California.

My life has made quite a few full circles, and it is simply remarkable that this is actually the church that I now have had a close relationship with for over 17 years. My experiences in high school that gave me friendships from all over the world taught me about apartheid and its antithesis to universal values. I am fortunate that here I am in adulthood and in America, basking in the presence of those who defeated apartheid with universal values.

Being a friend of All Saints in Pasadena wasn't something I sought out, it was a relationship that unfolded organically after the events of 9/11 rattled my faith in humanity. I was very shaken by the acts of terrorism in the name of Islam, and it was through an interfaith organization in Los Angeles, namely the Interfaith Communities United for Justice and Peace (ICUJP), that I found community, humanity, love, and compassion. One of its founders was Reverend George Regas whose gentle demeanor, calm, and loving ways brought me to the All Saints Church. It was then that I found out about its rebellious nature and how it had championed against apartheid, and maintained its deep ties to South Africa until now.

Over the years, I recognized that the values of the church intertwined with mine. As a friend of the church, I have spoken on various panels and have even delivered sermons at Sunday service. Invitations to their Christmas service are something I cherish, as this is a service that includes a rabbi reading from the Torah and a Muslim reading from the Quran about Mary and the birth of Jesus, or Prophet Isa to Muslims. When my faith in humanity depleted again with the ongoing genocide in Gaza, this is where I attend Christmas service to replenish a hollowed-out spirit.

Many years ago, I was elated when the then-Reverend Ed Bacon invited and introduced me to Reverend Bishop Desmond Tutu at a Sunday church service. Having grown up around dignitaries and heads of state, I don't get starstruck very easily, but in the presence of this iconic rebel, a good troublemaker, I felt an overwhelming mix of awe and giddiness. It was an unforgettable moment, and I will forever remember his demeanor, his humbleness, humor and captivating smile. He was a joy to be around, because he was the manifestation of joy and love.

The historical context that influences the spectrum of opinions from being in favor or against issues like apartheid and colonization continues to resonate in today's global politics. Whether it be the ongoing power struggle between the West and Russia, the legacy of slavery in the Americas, the genocide of Native Americans, the colonization of Palestine by European Jews, or the artificial division of the African continent into artificial borders, they are all being played out today. As an Asian from a colonized country, I get it. I have a profound empathy for the enduring struggles faced by the oppressed simply to be free, and sadly the world is full of the oppressed. For me, my father's generation's struggle to be free from British colonization is still vivid. Their drive, passion and aspirations are similar emotions I see in the people I meet and work with, and so are the arrogance of the oppressors I come across.

My experience being called "colored" as a child in London pales in comparison to what my friend Zimpande and the millions of others endured. It informed me that the concept of "colored" and its various forms of prejudice is bigger than that British boy's condescending attitude.

At the British School in New Delhi, Zimpande's best friends were White, Jewish twin boys Chris and Andrew Hall, also expelled from South Africa, whose parents were journalists and hardened anti-apartheid advocates. It was these Black and White South African friends that sealed my understanding of people, and that is, just because you are White does not mean you are anti-Black or prejudiced.

Many decades later while visiting Zimpande and his wife Afrika in Johannesburg, I was invited to his father's home for dinner. As MPV was starting to get requests for chapter affiliation in numerous countries, I asked him for advice on how to manage such a network. He smiled and responded, "Oh no, no, not so easy! We were focused on one man, one woman, one vote. The Muslim world is so diverse, billions of people, with billions of ideas and directions!" I smiled, and we toasted to that.

Another friend at The British School who brings a smile to my face is Mahmud, he was older than me and really tall. He was one of my table tennis sparring partners, and I remember how we would conspire to get to school extra early in the mornings to monopolize the table. His father was the Afghan ambassador to India, and the grandson of the Afghan king. Then suddenly, one day at school, he was gone. I have no idea what happened to him. I was told that with the Taliban 1.0 takeover of Afghanistan, his family was killed and because his father was the ambassador, it meant they no longer had diplomatic status. Many decades later, the Talibans still plague Afghanistan. Until today, whenever I pick up a ping-pong racket, he crosses my mind, and I wonder where he is. I remember him because of how much fun, laughter, and competitiveness we had with each other. When I smashed, he would smash the ball back, and before long we had the hallway full of spectators cheering us on. What a memorable way to start a school day, and it is this emotional memory of playing with Mahmud that shapes the way I view Afghan men, minus the Taliban.

People should be judged by their character, and nothing else.

***

The strong-willed spirit I cultivated during my youth in New Delhi was further honed on American soil. In my college years, I embraced the discipline of fasting during the Islamic month of Ramadan. As a minority, it built up my mental strength, which I attributed to my steely, unwavering, and obstinate attitude. My mother would call me "stubborn," but I have always seen it as perseverance and strength. This determination propelled me through the challenges of school, work, creative pursuits, and well, life!

While fasting, whether it was school, my job at the cafeteria dishing out food to fellow college mates, or working out before breaking fast, I would put my utmost energy into what I was doing. Sometimes friends who were fasting with me would tease, "Are you really fasting Ani?" In an evaluation written by a professor at my college, she wrote "good energy but sometimes spreads herself too thin. She needs to learn to prioritize." Regardless of how hot the weather was, playing soccer was a commitment, and so was fasting during Ramadan. So, I would push through and continue with both, each providing me with a different satisfaction—one for the body, the other for the soul.

My college days at Northern Illinois University also introduced me to a unique camaraderie of friends who shared my enthusiasm for sports activities and cultural background. One of my memorable Ramadans was during the hot and humid summer days in Illinois, when *maghrib*, or dusk, which is the time when we break our fast, wasn't until 9:30 p.m., a good 17 hours without food or water. My pack of friends: Uddin, Nazri, Sallahuddin, Zainal, Nordin, and Zul, all guys—and I would go out for a good 30-minute run through the town of DeKalb before going back to one of the apartments of a college mate to break our fast, first with lots of water, and followed by food. The cooking was always such a feast of Malay dishes. Since Malay dishes are laden with carbohydrates, not to mention it being a late-night meal, it made the workouts and running necessary. It was exhilarating to be soaking with sweat, exhausted by the heat and thirst, and then getting that first sip of water. It is this act of limiting yourself that forces us to appreciate that drop of water and to empathize with those who don't even know if and when their thirst can be quenched.

These experiences of pushing myself to the limits and the exhilarating emotion and moments of accomplishment—no matter how big or small—are what enrich our lives. It was also what prepared me for real life after college.

*** 

In Los Angeles, my journey took a turn toward the pursuit of my passion: songwriting. While waitressing to sustain myself, paying my dues, as they say, I dedicated my afternoons and evenings to honing my craft. The discipline instilled in me during fasting became a guiding force, I found my hunger helped me remain focused, hungry not just for food but for what I want to achieve in life, which was to make it as a songwriter. The rigorous routine of balancing work, songwriting, and self-study was a discipline ingrained in me as a child, trained not to waste time and that every minute of the day was precious time to be used wisely.

My daily routine began at 6 a.m., waitressing from 6:30 a.m. to 2:30 p.m. Once at home, I would take a 15-minute catnap to refresh, and then I spent many hours songwriting, trying out new arrangements and perfecting programming skills. I taught myself how to work with the new "midi" technology of that time, where different sets of instruments could be synchronized to play a set of sounds, controlled by a "controller" or computer. I would spend hours working on tracks, my many years of piano training and the experience of playing different instruments helped with composing and programming different musical parts, and my habit of listening to music for its arrangements and production for as long as I can remember, were all coalescing.

Even with a college degree, I opted for waitressing rather than a straight nine to five job. With a straight job I wasn't earning enough income to pay rent and save money, let alone have the time to be creative. In other words, a straight nine to five job rendered me broke. By the time I had to get dressed up in business attire, drive in traffic to and from work, I had consumed a total of ten hours of my day, without any energy or clarity of mind to be creative in the evenings. If I was going to go for a corporate job, I might as well have moved back to Malaysia where I had my network of college friends, and family to help.

Before I landed on waitressing, I signed up as a maid. I went from having maids to becoming a maid. I was in Los Angeles, in my mid-twenties, a university graduate and yet so lost and alone. With every stroke scrubbing a tub, I thought of the housekeepers I had growing up, reinforcing the appreciation for the comfortable life I was privileged with. And with every stroke, I also knew my parents would not have approved of this job I've taken.

But, never will I ever ask for a handout. Never.

I was always self-assured, there was nothing I couldn't do if I set my mind to it, and my father always encouraged me to "aim for the moon." And I did, but here I was wiping someone else's dust, and it contributed to drowning myself in self-doubt, a state of mind that was very foreign to me.

Throughout those few months, I always thought my father would turn in his grave if he knew. I kept my struggles to myself and never told my mother or anyone. Writing about it now is my first public testimonial.

This snippet of my life, of struggle to make ends meet, of the determination to achieve your dreams only reinforced my empathy for others, for those who have struggled all their lives for the basics of life.

\*\*\*

In 1985, at Monmouth College, a girls' soccer team was nonexistent. This failed to deter my aspirations. Yes, so presumptuous and audacious as a newbie in America to tell the coach, "Since we don't have a girls team, I'd like to try out for the boys team." I am sure the coach was taken aback, but he acquiesced, and thus began my stint as the lone girl on the team, serving as a substitute for a season. When I transferred to Northern Illinois University for my second year in college in 1982, I tried out for the girls' team and got in. With a double degree in Economics and Political Science, my world revolved around academics and soccer; that was all I had time for. Music fell by the wayside, until a dislocated kneecap put my soccer playing days to an abrupt end.

Immersed in the swift rhythm of soccer, for decades I never had the patience for American sports, be it football or baseball. Baseball, in particular, bored me with its slow pace and prolonged periods of standing around—quite the opposite of soccer's continuous intensity, paused only by injuries or halftime. I harbored doubts about a baseball player's ability to match the physical endurance demanded of a soccer player.

Yet my journey into the realm of American sports, particularly baseball, unfolded gradually. In the passing years, my husband immersed himself in watching the Dodgers game, dedicating hours to it while working out. The COVID era, which grounded me from traveling, turned out to be a period of newfound time. It was during these COVID years that I delved into the intricacies of the game, finding joy in the ceaseless and informative commentary, the lively organ tunes, the snippets of pop songs between plays, and, of course, the players' personalized walk-on songs. A walk-on song! What other sport boasts such a unique tradition? I've now proudly embraced my Dodgers fandom. With closed eyes, I can distinguish whether a game is at the Dodger Stadium or during an away match—the Dodgers home game with its distinctive, cheerful vibe. Unlike fans of opposing teams chanting "beat LA," the Dodgers' supporters echo a more positive mantra: "go Dodgers." This resonates with my life philosophy— no need to diminish others to elevate oneself; just do well.

As for football, my only interest is in the ever mesmerizing halftime show, a spectacle of unparalleled production quality. Be it baseball, football, or basketball, there's no denying that America excels in delivering top-notch entertainment. This, to me, encapsulates the essence of American culture. If we can't talk about money, politics or religion, well, all that's left is sports and entertainment!

***

For 23 years, I maintained my permanent residency status in America. The thought of becoming an American citizen, however, brought a dilemma—that of surrendering my Malaysian passport. American politicians failed to inspire me, and I found the country's foreign policies riddled with hypocrisy on many levels. Sadly, nothing has changed on that front.

Then came Barack Hussein Obama. The first time I heard him speak was at the Democratic National Convention in 2004, and I sensed that paying attention to him was imperative. One day after he declared his presidential candidacy, I filed my papers for American citizenship because this was the one candidate who moved me to do so. Surprisingly, my citizenship process took only a few months. During the interview, upon reviewing my 23 years of residency, the officer exclaimed, "What took you so long!"

While Obama had his accomplishments, disappointments became evident. It crystallized that irrespective of the president, foreign policies underwent minimal change. It may be by a few degrees in either direction, unless you're Trump, then in that case, you can share top-secret documents with America's enemy, plan for an insurrection of Congress, monetize your name brand in the hundreds of millions of dollars, and still be a free man.

As my work became more visible nationally and internationally, I somehow found myself on President Obama's list for an invitation to an *iftar* dinner. It was an exquisite sit-down dinner, with French service, featuring a table of eight. I was seated beside Susan Rice, Obama's national security adviser. My other fellow diners included ambassadors from Egypt, who went to the same Port Said School I did in Zamalek; Rashida Tlaib, who was at that time a Michigan state legislator; and Imam Mohammad Magid, a prominent religious leader in the DC area and Virginia. I was in good company, and we had a vibrant conversation.

This was the first time I met the imam, and I enjoyed a friendly banter with him. The imam was talking about his interfaith work, and how he took religious leaders, especially imams to Auschwitz to educate them about the Holocaust. With a teasing smile, I interjected, "I'm an imam too; how come I've never been invited?" Susan's head spun around, stunned at the idea of a female imam, and we proceeded to chat a bit about MPV's inclusive and egalitarian structure and our values.

As dinner wound down, Obama made his rounds, taking group photos with the guests at each table. As he came by our table, he extended his hand to me, and I greeted him with "apa khabar," in Malay, which is "hello," or more literally "What's the news!" I figured that would be one way I would stand out. He was pleasantly surprised by my Bahasa, and I got a few words in about MPV, to which he responded, "We need your progressive voices in this world." He stood beside me to pose for photos, and I put my arms around him, something I do with most people, by the way, which surprised him, and he reciprocated with arms around his guests on both sides.

Meeting presidents, prime ministers, and royalty due to my father's merit was not unfamiliar, but I never imagined that taking an oath as an American inspired by Obama would lead to invitations to the White House based on the merits of my work. Since then, I've been to the White House on multiple occasions. Each occasion is an exhibit of gracious hosting, respect for its guests, and an acknowledgment and acceptance of the diversity of America, which is what makes the idea of "America" exceptional.

Reflecting on my experiences, I recognize the quintessential American spirit of individuality and entrepreneurship. This freedom to express oneself, unencumbered by societal constraints, is a defining feature of American culture. It contrasts sharply with the limitations imposed by some cultures that discourage individuality and prize conformity. As I now work on human rights and social justice issues, I see distinctive mental barriers curtailed by different cultures and their societies. In my own upbringing, as an example, I did not have the right to think freely, there was always a limit. This limit also exists in communities within American society, and it is this curtailing of freedom to think that limits an individual's full potential. All one needs to do is look at the number of patents registered in a country, and it will most likely correlate with a society that nurtures the right to think freely, and differently.

Even in Europe, there are some expressions that are prohibited as it goes against the well-being of the society at large. And in many Western societies, being an individual, "standing out" is sometimes frowned upon, and discouraged.

The Dutch have a saying "Wie als dubbeltje wordt geboren, wordt nooit een kwartje" which translates to "He who is born a dime will never become a quarter," meaning you are defined by your lineage. Similarly, like much of the world, you are defined by the status of your family name, whether you have a title in front of your name, like a "lord," "sir," what your forefathers did defines your pedigree, if you will. In some societies, it is the tribe, and in others, it is the caste system.

In America, you can recreate yourself. You are encouraged to "think outside the box," "be yourself," and Nike's "just do it" are just a few phrases that have shaped this unique American psyche. You can even register your name as "doing business as," or a DBA, where your individuality is a business unto itself. That's classic American.

As an immigrant, my husband and I embody the essence of the American Dream. We come from very different upbringings and cultural backgrounds, but we both have outsized ambitions and drive.

When starting a business, it was not just an expression of individual thought and creativity, there were also bureaucratic hurdles, which was a learning curve. The first store location my husband and his partner started was a family affair. We painted the walls, helped with cleaning, and even our then four-year-old daughter helped out. It's what makes us a three-person team to this day. Our American Dream is a herculean feat, filled with very hard work, sheer grit, no rich family to fund our endeavors, no trust fund, or mentor to show us the way. Our success has been uniquely ours. Contrary to the Dutch saying, we excelled to become a "dollar."

Given my upbringing and the amalgamation of cultures and beliefs, there were moments of personal transformation. Cultural norms that once defined my identity began to fade as I embraced the liberating essence of American life. In a conversation with my Dutch husband recently, he shared how as a young boy, he and his soccer teammates would always shower in the nude and nobody thought anything of it. Now, there is a new phenomenon taking place in the Netherlands, where boys from the Muslim faith shower with their underwear on, which, by default, is making the native Dutch boys feel "bare."

This triggered something deep within me that I had completely forgotten. I also used to bathe with my underwear on!

As a child bathing with my younger brother, and as a preteen being bathed by our caregivers, and into adulthood, and even in the privacy of my own bathroom, I always wore underwear when I showered!

In habitual form, during my first shower upon moving into my dorm in America, I wore my underwear. The shower was a fully enclosed unit in a shared bathroom, so privacy was not an issue. Upon finishing up with the shower it dawned on me I had nowhere to hang my wet underwear!

Lo and behold, this habit of 18 years changed within the first week of arriving for college in the US. The first few weeks felt really strange, showering without underwear on, feeling water on my skin where I hadn't before, and feeling really naked. This was one of the many changes I came to experience, cultural habits I began to shed as I became more "American."

In the tapestry of my life, these diverse threads have woven a narrative of resilience, cultural fusion, introspection, and unwavering determination. Each experience, whether on the soccer field, in the creative realm, or within the confines of cultural norms, has contributed to who I have become. Through these moments of life lessons, there is a common thread— observing, learning, and challenging myself into becoming an individual shaped by the intersection of cultures, boundless aspirations, and an unyielding spirit to chart my own course in the world.

***

# 10
# Interfaith marriages

When I first started the progressive community in Los Angeles in 2006, my primary desire was simple: to establish a welcoming space for Muslims, particularly those in mixed families like mine—a space where we could debate openly and partake in the arts. I wanted a place where my non-Muslim husband wouldn't be shunned, and I would not be condemned to hell for marrying a non-Muslim because I was living in "sin." Little did I anticipate that this community would evolve into a hub for all sorts of Muslims, including Muslims in interfaith marriages, challenging societal norms and bridging diverse traditions.

As the community grew, I was being sought out and asked to conduct interfaith Islamic marriages where non-Muslim partners did not have to convert. This was not something I had envisioned or planned for, but it was and still is clear that an interfaith Islamic marriage that adheres to the teachings of the Qur'an is very much a need and something that is growing in demand.

Imams in America officially refuse to officiate interfaith marriages without the conversion of the non-Muslim partner. The rejection of such unions highlights the conservative stance prevalent in many religious circles. I found that out for myself when I was getting married to my non-Muslim Dutch husband in 1990. University chaplains, comparatively, are more open-minded, a few officiate non-conversion interfaith Islamic marriages, untethered from conservative influence.

The reason chaplains attached to universities are more open to conducting non-conversion interfaith Islamic marriages is because their practice is not beholden to conservative paymasters and therefore has more freedom to practice an Islam that is more truthful to the Quran.

An Islamic marriage is often coined as *nikah,* which in Arabic means sexual intercourse. Sorry to be crude, but this is a reality check—especially for many non-Arabic speaking Muslims.

The *nikah* contract, or marriage contract, is therefore one that stipulates the terms of a licit sexual relationship, because marriage, according to the Quran, is a commitment and contract between two individuals of sound mind. You have to be of sound mind to enter into a contract, and you have to be mature or an adult to negotiate a contractual agreement. For centuries, and until today in some tribes and in Hindu marriages, women are largely considered properties to be owned. Women had to adopt the religion and culture of the husband, and it is assumed that the children will automatically adopt the religion of the father. The marriage contract was the Quran's way of upending this deeply entrenched misogynistic culture, giving women leverage to negotiate their rights in marriage as stipulated in the agreement.

For example, in the marriage contract, the woman can stipulate the terms of the marriage such as the right to visit her family, the right to work outside the home, the right to own property and to manage it, and the right to practice her religion, all rights given to women in the 700s AD in the Quran. Incidentally, European women didn't have the right to own property until 1870, and American women didn't have the right to open their own bank account until 1974. Just sayin'!

Unfortunately though, patriarchal and tribal interpretations of Islam are still the prism through which the religion is practiced and are the basis for why religious leaders and imams prohibit Muslim women from marrying non-Muslims. They still preach that the children will become non-Muslim, and that the women are weak and will "follow the husband's demands." As part of my officiating service, I also educate couples and their families. When I explain the historical context for why American imams largely prohibit Muslim women from marrying non-Muslim men, it inevitably ends up being an "aha" moment.

American and European imams assume women of the 21st century, especially those in the West, are weak and unprincipled. The reality contradicts their assumptions. Based on my many years of observation, when a Muslim woman marries a non-Muslim man, the child usually ends up being raised as Muslim. And when a Muslim man marries a non-Muslim woman, the child is likely to adopt the faith of the mother. This has direct bearing on the fact, that in most cases—even in our modern society, the mother is still the main caregiver and therefore the main influencer on the child. This debunks one of the illogical rationales for prohibiting the Muslim woman from marrying non-Muslim men.

This question of what religion your child is going to be raised with is a hang-up shared by other orthodox and conservative religions as well.

The nuances and contradictions of religious leaders kept coming to my attention from couples that come to me to officiate their interfaith Islamic marriages. Regardless of what their religious background is, young Muslim women and men are adamant about marrying within the Islamic tradition while vehemently opposing the forced conversion that mosques and sometimes families require of their non-Muslim partners. They believe stating the declaration of faith to Islam, the *shahada*, for the purpose of marriage would be a lie, insincere, and would diminish the dignity of such a declaration. I agree and would go further to say, it is nothing short of hypocrisy.

There are plenty of examples from old Muslim traditions to draw from that free me to support and conduct interfaith marriages. For example, during Prophet Muhammad's days, women were the first to convert to Islam, and they were allowed to marry and stay married to their non-Muslim husbands. Plus, there is no prohibition for women to marry outside the faith in the Quran. Prophet Muhammad's daughter Zainab was married to a pagan, and she remained married to him even after she converted to Islam. When Muslims immigrated to Medina for safety from the Meccan pagan tribes—who had starved them as a collective punishment, and who had made several attempts to assassinate Prophet Muhammad—Zainab remained in Mecca with her husband rather than immigrating to Medina with her father.

If Prophet Muhammad didn't force Zainab to divorce her pagan husband or force him to convert to Islam, then it goes to show, the 21st century practice of prohibiting Muslim women from marrying non-Muslim men has no basis in Islam.

Over the past 17 years, I have officiated countless interfaith Islamic marriages responding to the growing demand as more and more Muslims choose partners outside their faith. This is indicative of the statistics mirroring this shift, where the majority of marriages in the US are of mixed faith and mixed race.

In the early days, the interfaith marriages I conducted were intimate affairs, often held discreetly in non-Muslim family backyards, with maybe a Muslim sibling present for support. Today, these unions are celebrated extravagantly. The change is stark with destination weddings such as Cancun, and with large members of the Muslim family present as well.

I vividly recall my first interfaith marriage ceremony in 2007—a poignant event where a Muslim woman married a non-Muslim man of the Christian tradition. It was held in the backyard of the groom's parents' home, with a guest list of about 15 people, mostly from the groom's side of the family, and one sibling from the Muslim bride's side of the family in attendance. Despite the joy, I sensed the sadness in her eyes, a result of her parents' absence due to their disapproval. I still remember that feeling. I have seen that heavy heart and sadness too many times over the years illustrating the challenges faced by those who defy traditional expectations.

On so many occasions, when I answered phone calls for MPV, and a bride inquired if I would marry them Islamically and

I responded affirmatively, some would burst into tears of relief and happiness. This highlights the trauma and emotional coercion that many face from parents, the burden of not "sinning" and going to hell, all gone, lifted, vaporized, dispelled with a simple "yes."

As a firm advocate of religious freedom, in my Islamic interfaith services I make sure to remind Muslims of the meaning of this verse, "There is no compulsion in religion" (Quran 2:256). It is for this reason that I don't buckle when pressured to convert non-Muslims against his or her free will. Converting to Islam is simple; with conviction in your heart all one has to do is utter the declaration of faith "there is no god but God, and Prophet Muhammad as his messenger." But on many occasions, this declaration is uttered under pretense just to please the Muslim family, or for the Muslim family to "save face" that their child has not broken an "Islamic rule" by marrying a non-Muslim. Confronting instances of parents pressuring for conversion, I emphasize the hypocrisy of such demands, urging them to embrace honesty rather than perpetuate a facade.

The fact that there is no prohibition against marrying outside the faith, the conversion becomes the perfect example of fakery, religious hypocrisy at its best. On a few occasions even after agreeing to a no-conversion marriage, I have found myself accosted by a Muslim parent asking me to make the non-Muslim utter the declaration of faith. At this point, I lecture the parents about hypocrisy, and they back off.

Some years ago, after conducting a wedding service at one large interfaith marriage in Los Angeles, the mother of the bride came up and asked me if I could do a sermon justifying the legitimacy of such an interfaith service. This was to rebut the grumbling she was hearing from pockets of the conservative Muslim family in attendance.

So before dinner was served, in an impromptu sermon, I addressed the subject matter at hand. "Asking the non-Muslim groom to convert to Islam against his freewill just to please 'you' so that you can save face in your community is the height of hypocrisy."

I continued, "We recite *surah al-fatiha* multiple times a day. In it we ask that we lead a straight path, which means a path of truth and honesty. Instead of asking this young couple to start their lives with a lie, we should all be commending them for their forthrightness, and for not succumbing to a forced conversion, which in itself, is against the teachings of the Quran."

I sat down for dinner.

A few minutes later, two elderly couples came up to thank me for reminding them of the meaning of *al-fatihah*, which is a little bit like the Lord's Prayer, by the way, and that the service I provided helped them keep their younger generation within the faith as they both said almost in unison:

"We are starting to lose them."

I thanked them for their humbleness and kind words.

And then a young man came along and challenged me on the permissibility of such an interfaith Islamic marriage.

To which I said, "Go back to the Quran, find me the verse that prohibits it and then come back and talk to me." He never did come back.

Imams and officiants who partake in such fake conversions and pretend as if it is legitimate have no moral grounding. They cheapen the meaning of conviction, which, to a convert, could only mean that these Muslims around him that he is marrying into are just unprincipled. So dominant is the notion that a Muslim woman must marry a Muslim man that young Muslim women, under a lot of duress, succumb to these cultural pressures, hiring a traditional imam, therefore male, to officiate this façade, therefore, promoting patriarchy for the next generation.

The weddings I conduct are not marriages arranged by parents and family members. Arranged marriages tend to match partners to the same tribe, class, and caste designed to protect one's tribal character, after all, God forbid if your child marries an "untouchable," a nonbeliever, a "black," or whoever that family heritage has deemed as "the other." This type of tribalist thinking is, of course at the other end of the spectrum from the marriages I officiate. The marriages I conduct break all the traditional rules designed to confine us in our tiny boxes.

When the challenges against a couple marrying are very intense, the forces are usually from the parents and extended families. A Muslim-Hindu marriage can be very challenging because of the political climate in India. Yes, international politics can be a heavy influence on an intimate relationship between two souls here in America. The rise of Hindutva and the toxic misinformation about Islam and Hinduism are designed to drive these two communities in India apart, when historically this was not the case. Theologically, there are many similar philosophical concepts between the two religions. To help couples and families overcome their respective prejudices of the other, one of MPV's officiants, Mike Ghouse, developed a booklet to draw the similarities of these two faiths as a tool for families to understand and overcome prejudices of each other.

Similarly, officiating Muslim-Jewish weddings can be a challenge, mostly due to political reasons as well. We share so many similarities between the two faith traditions, but you wouldn't know it from some of the hateful rhetoric. Over the years most of the Muslim-Jewish weddings I officiated have been in our inclusive Muslim tradition, no conversion, and in the presence of the inner circles of both sides of the family, with the exception of Nisha and Matt.

This Muslim-Jewish wedding of Nisha and Matt on September 3, 2023, in Creston, California, was a memorable one because I co-officiated it with a female Rabbi Janice Mehring. Together we created a seamless wedding service that represented both traditions without compromising either. This weaving could only have been possible with a co-officiant void of ego, and one who is genuinely inclusive. I found this spirit in Rabbi Janice, and I'm sure she felt the same for me as we hit it off right away.

We started off the interfaith marriage service with the Jewish *Ketubah*—the signing of the Jewish marriage contract in Hebrew and English at the top of the service, and bookmarked the ending of the service with the signing of the Islamic marriage contract in Arabic and English. The service was mostly in English, and where there were Hebrew readings by Rabbi Janice, I read the English translations, and when I recited in Arabic, Rabbi Janice read the English translations. We ended with everyone calling out "Malzatov", "Alhamdulillah," and "Congratulations" all together! It was a cacophony of sounds and languages not usually heard in a celebratory manner. It was also heartwarming to see this young couple make such an effort to bring the two traditions, the two sides of families and friends, together. They were playing their part toward creating a new American culture, and I am so happy to be part of creating this new interfaith marriage culture.

In continuing with a celebratory theme, I have also officiated large and elaborate Muslim-Hindu interfaith Islamic marriages at destination weddings, where the groom arrived on a horse while the Hindu family and friends danced their way to an infectious percussion player, to meet the Muslim bride's family members. At this wedding, I co-officiated the ceremony with a pandit, a Hindu priest. A Hindu marriage is very elaborate, with a fire pit at its center, and with each section of the service having meaningful symbols of what it represents. Weaving in a Muslim-Hindu service is very difficult, and after a few of these, I've surrendered to it having to be a complete entity of its own, starting with the Hindu service and with the pandit then turning over the couple to me for the Islamic part, and with both of us pronouncing the couple husband and wife, or at another Muslim-Hindu wedding, "wife and wife."

Conducting same-sex and interfaith marriages does not just bring people of two different faith or cultural backgrounds together but it facilitates love between couples where, sometimes, families still cannot accept their LGBTQ+ child.

At a large same-sex interfaith wedding in Memphis between Hennah, a woman of Afghan heritage, and Renee, a woman of African American heritage, the wedding was deeply rooted in Islamic tradition, with the bride confirming that she is marrying out of her own free will and that a *mehr* has been agreed to as stated in the Islamic marriage contract. To be inclusive of the Christian family, I invited the African American mother to read the First Letter of Saint Paul to the Corinthians, which reads:

"Love is patient; love is kind. Love is not jealous, it does not put on airs, and it is not snobbish. Love is never rude, it is not self-seeking, it is not prone to anger; neither does it brood over injuries. Love does not rejoice in what is wrong but rejoices with the truth. There is no limit to love's forbearance, to its trust, its hope, its power to endure."

I followed up this reading with a recitation about marriage in the Quran, verse 30:21, first in Arabic and followed by the English translation, which reads:

"Among Her proofs is that She created for you spouses from among yourselves, in order to have tranquility and contentment with each other, and She placed in your hearts love and care toward your spouses. In this, there are sufficient proofs for people who think."

The interfaith marriages I create anchor the religious requirement but weave in the many traditions in our multiracial and multicultural society.

At a time in America when the enslaved were prohibited from marrying legally, jumping over the broom was their way of symbolizing their marriage. So, to end this wedding service, as a broom-bearer, I placed the broom on the ground for Renee and Hennah to jump over it hand in hand, their wedding gowns trailing. It was such a beautiful sight.

My heart was full.

These unions truly embody the spirit of America—unified by common values of respect and inclusivity. These couples forge their paths, transcending cultural, religious, and racial boundaries. By facilitating such unions, it reinforces my core belief in love, and in having the freedom to marry who you love, free from regressive cultures and their constraints. And through MPV, we have scaled up these core values, promoting an inclusive tradition, defying the confines of matchmaking based on tribe, caste, or religion. As the creator and designer of such a marriage, I am constantly filled with gratitude and satisfaction that I have enabled happiness and fought against exclusionary mindsets and traditions.

Whenever I feel disheartened by the division in American society and the numerous conflicts around the world, I think of the inclusive marriages and traditions we have created and facilitated at the micro and individual level. The female South Asian Muslim doctor marrying a male White Christian nurse; the South Asian Muslim female lawyer marrying a South Asian

Hindu male corporate executive; the Muslim female in IT marrying a Hindu male also in IT; the Arab Muslim woman marrying a Jewish man, or a Shi'a Muslim woman marrying a Baha'i
man are just some of the different weddings I've officiated.
Remembering their happy faces reminds me of my contribution to creating an inclusive society, that American melting
pot, which I believe will eventually and permanently do away
with the hate mongering.

***

# 11
# LGBTQ+ rights

In 2007, California found itself embroiled in a contentious battle on same-sex marriage. As an ally and supporter of LGBTQ+ folks, I firmly believe in equal rights for all citizens, because we are not a theocracy. Whether you believe homosexuality is permissible or not, in Islam or whatever your belief system is, is irrelevant. One's belief or nonbelief is a private matter.

In the aftermath of 9/11, when mosques and Islamic centers were under attack, and death threats directed at Muslims abound, it was the progressive faith institutions that took a stand to protect these spaces. In Los Angeles, Interfaith Communities United for Justice and Peace (ICUJP) organized a human chain in the rain, a group of over 50 people holding hands, creating a symbolic protective barrier around the Islamic Center of Southern California.

However, during the Proposition 8 campaign, which aimed to ban same-sex marriage in California, reversing what was already legal, some conservative elements, including the Islamic Shura Council of Southern California, endorsed the initiative. In contrast, progressive churches and synagogues opposed Proposition 8.

Behind the scenes, the Shura Council, an organization made up of a coalition of Islamic centers and mosques in Southern California called for their congregations and constituencies to vote in favor of Proposition 8 and prominently promoted their position on their website. As a proponent of non-discrimination and equality, I stood solo on this issue. I had no sway with the conservative Muslim communities; however, the progressive churches and synagogues did. There was one person I knew who did, my friend, the late George Regas, who at that time was the rector at All Saints in Pasadena and a co-founder of ICUJP.

It was George Regas, with his close friend Rabbi Leonard Beerman, who talked things over with the late Maher Hathout, who at that time was an influential community leader at the Islamic Center of Southern California and a member of the Shura Council. Regas' persuasive argument was "we Christians and Jews stood by the Muslim community after 9/11, protecting you, defending you against discrimination, and now you are advocating for the discrimination of gay members of our communities."

The outcome of that meeting resulted in the Shura Council taking down their public instruction for their constituency to vote "yes" on Proposition 8 from their website.

The Muslim attitude toward homosexuality will never change if religious teachers keep pumping out homophobic teachings, poisoning and promoting hate from an early age. So wired is this hate that an acquaintance, a Tunisian LGBTQ+ advocate, Ahmed Ben Amor, shared this rather humorous but daunting sad story with me:

In a village deep in the interior of Tunisia, Ahmed attempted to persuade an old man against his deep disdain for homosexuality. He recalled how the old man said, "Even if Prophet Muhammad was to come down here in front of me and tell me that it is not a sin to be a homosexual and Muslim, I would not believe it!" The harmful impact of such teachings is evident in this story, illustrating the deeply ingrained homophobia that persists.

A theology promoting hate is not benign, it causes real harm to those on the receiving end of that discrimination. When family members, and especially parents, emotionally and physically abuse their homosexual child because the religious teachers and leaders condemn them, the suffering endured by LGBTQ+ folks angers me. When a child has been raised to believe they are going to hell for being gay, it is devastating, traumatizing, and causes self-hatred, depression, and mental health issues. I know this, as I have seen and have been the "mother" for some young LGBTQ+ youth who need validation and affirmation of their identity. Yet, I have also witnessed the opposite scenario and seen the positive impact of what an affirming and loving message has on one's well-being.

In 2016, Omar Mateen killed 49 innocent partygoers at the Pulse Club in Orlando. This heinous act was perpetrated by someone imbued with self-hate. All over the world, including in the West, there are too many imams preaching hate, not just of homosexuality and trans folks but of "the other," whoever they choose the other to be. Derogatory preachings by Sunnis of Shia, Shia of Sunnis, of "the Jews," of Black folks, of women being inferior and needing to be controlled, and so on. It is for this reason we started the #NoHateInMyFaith campaign.

When a young man in our community expressed his depression and the emotional and mental abuse he was suffering at the hands of his parents, we welcomed him with open hearts and with lots of love. On one occasion, I asked him to give the sermon for our community Eid prayer, for a community that was mixed with straight, gay and trans folks. To be given such a spiritual leadership role is healing, and heal he did! Soon after, he left our community, flew off into the world, and I'm confident he's doing well.

Seeing how healing it is for LGBTQ+ Muslims to be affirmed of their identities in the language of Islam, I saw the need to develop resources for this community. In partnership with a Muslim scholar of Islam, Dr Scott Siraj Al-Haqq Kugle, and with support from Human Rights Campaign and Carpenter Foundation, I secured the funds to produce the contents that till today, I know have lifted people up and saved lives.

The many messages we receive from LGBTQ+ Muslims about how MPV's contents have saved them from depression, given them hope, or instilled value in their identity, and that they no longer thought of suicide as an option, is extremely gratifying. I am not saying the language of faith can replace mental health counseling, but what I am saying is that I have seen how a loving and compassionate language of faith helps those who just need someone to believe in their human dignity.

After the Pulse shooting, imams and religious leaders scrambled to declare, "We support LGBTQ+ rights." It was a sudden pivot, an attempt to distance themselves from the responsibility of promoting homophobic theology in their communities by co-opting human rights language. Despite their public statements, the inclusive rhetoric wasn't and still isn't reflected in the theology taught at mosques and religious schools.

In 2017, following the affirming messages for LGBTQ+ rights by Muslim religious leaders, the Human Rights Campaign (HRC), one of America's largest LGBTQ+ civil society organizations, decided to reserve a table at the annual ISNA conference. HRC invited MPV to partner with them and I said, "Of course but, be forewarned, don't expect to be welcomed." In our application, we were transparent about our organizational mission and vision, and what we stood for.

As the event unfolded, our table was set with our brochures, booklets and banners. Attending the table on behalf of MPV was Frank Parmir, and Michael Toumayan for HRC. Attendees approached with questions about LGBTQ+ rights in Islam and women-led prayer, offering support and affirmation for our inclusive interpretation of Islam. However, a young man, beard to the chest with ankle-length pants, looked at our contents and frowned, picked up a few materials, and left.

Soon after, a security guard approached, instructing us to pack up and leave within an hour. Frank, panicking, called me for advice. I told him to pack up but insisted they not leave until meeting with the person who made that decision and who instructed the guard to tell you.

"What will happen, Frank, is that ISNA will deny it, and they will claim the messenger misunderstood and passed on the wrong message. I know the games they play. Whatever you do, insist on speaking to the decision maker and I repeat, do not leave the building without doing so."

Frank and Michael were escorted to an office room by a security guard to meet with Basharat Saleem, the conference director of the ISNA convention. At the back of the room, a few unidentified men observed and didn't intervene in the meeting. Michael asked Basharat what was the problem as our organizations' missions were clearly outlined in the application.

Basharat responded, "We don't have a problem with HRC, we just have a problem with MPV."

Michael said, "Excuse me? What do you mean?"

Basharat said, "We don't have a problem with HRC but we have a problem with MPV because it is a Muslim organization supporting LGBT."

When Michael relayed this to me, I couldn't help but smile. It was a stark confirmation of the warned-of hypocrisy that I had cautioned him and other progressive organizations about for years.

"Well now, you have experienced it, and heard it firsthand!"

Fast forward to 2023, and the same imams and religious leaders, who once lied about supporting LGBTQ+ rights have now published a position statement claiming they were mistaken, asking God for forgiveness. Instead of embracing inclusion, they have aligned themselves with the Christian Right in their zealotry, vehemently opposing what they call the "gay agenda."

In a world full of hypocrites like those, there stands Imam Magid, unswayed and resolute.

Imam Magid is a prominent and influential religious leader in the Virginia and D.C. area with three megamosques. I teased him about learning from the Evangelical Christians and their megachurches. He's a sport and takes my needling with a smile. He is the same imam I met some years ago at President Obama's *iftar* in 2008, and we have remained in good standing. I invited him to be a participant at our #ImamsForShe panel at the UN in New York, and we've met at various State Department events and at various White House receptions on several occasions.

At a conference I spoke at Harvard University, Imam Magid was there as a fellow speaker, and I invited him for lunch for a private conversation. For Muslims, we were going through a tumultuous time with the height of ISIS. The murdering, pillaging, and thieving that God was supposed to have eradicated in the story of Prophet Lut as in the Quran, or Lot in the Bible, was now being conducted by this terrorist group. Along with those crimes, ISIS took Yazidi women as slaves, and took pleasure in killing, especially homosexuals in the most cruel and inhumane manner.

We ordered lunch, and I tried to say this in the most diplomatic and polite manner I could.

"Imam Magid, I have the deepest disdain for ISIS, but not far behind is my disdain for American imams. ISIS, they live by their conviction. They don't like gays, they kill them, push them off the building, and if they are still alive, they stone them to death." He gasped, stunned at such a demeaning comparison.

I continued, "American imams don't live by their conviction. What is their problem with homosexuality? Did Prophet Muhammad punish anyone for being a homosexual?"

He sat back, thought for a second, and responded, "No."

I continued, "Is there punishment in the Quran for being a homosexual?"

He responded, "No."

So, I closed the case with, "So what is the problem? Why can't they accept homosexuality in Islam?"

To which he nodded and said, "Yes, we need to be kind to our gay brothers and sisters."

He opened his talk at Harvard with, "I want to thank sister Ani Zonneveld for reminding me that we need to be kind to our gay brothers and sisters." I wasn't expecting this public acknowledgment, and I was floored by his humility because most conservative imams in America are arrogant and think they are God's gift. But public acknowledgment of the need to be kind to gay individuals, as voiced by Imam Magid, signified huge progress. I'm glad I did not hold back during our lunch conversation.

Most times after having such private conversations, I don't expect much to come of it. I know I've put it out there to the universe, and what comes next, or not, is beyond my control. However, one day I received an email from a young woman who came out to her dad as a lesbian. After several email exchanges, she shared that her dad spoke to his imam who explained there are different ways of understanding the story of Lot. Instead of reading it as condemnation of homosexuality, it can also be read as condemnation of inhospitality, violence, and rape, especially given that the rape victims included men, women, and girls. And it was because of this imam's counseling that he accepted his lesbian daughter. I asked, "What's the imam's name?" She said, "Imam Magid."

My heart was full.

Since I've been advocating for LGBTQ+ rights long before it was the cool thing to do, my name is out there as an advocate to the point that some folks assume I must be lesbian. So, now my biography includes "as an ally." In the early days of supporting LGBTQ+ rights, most Muslims both straight and gay didn't support my position. Straight Muslims thought I was going to hell for promoting homosexuality, and LGBTQ+ folks thought I was infringing on their "territory."

I'm not sure what is territorial about supporting human rights and dignity. From the start, my work has been intersectional. We are all intersectional and have multiple hyphenated identities, so the idea of working on one issue is selfish, and it doesn't do our collective causes any good. We all need allies. During 9/11, Muslims needed allies from non-Muslims to protect their lives. The reality is that we all need each other at one point or another.

In America, some under-aged young Muslim women in conservative communities are being forced into marriage, especially if they are found to be gay. This is a child's rights issue regardless of whether the child is straight or gay. It is an issue that should concern not only the anti-forced-marriage and anti-child-marriage advocates, but the LGBTQ+ rights activists as well, but it doesn't. Some activists are even territorial, with the small-mindedness of calling out potential allies to "stay in your own lane," as my friend and mentor Kevin Jennings experienced. Jennings is a white gay man and, at the time, co-chair of MPV's Board of Trustees, who defended me in the attacks I received from Ilhan Omar's fans. MPV's work has always been intersectional in nature drawing in diverse allyship. I am a strong believer in lifting everyone up together, though I admit sometimes it is too heavy of a lift.

At the UN, I hold panels and forums on a regular basis on various issues that we advocate for as a way to educate diplomats and fellow human rights defenders of our work. On one occasion in 2016, I co-organized a three-day forum, "Freedom of Religion and Belief and Sexuality," in partnership with the UN Special Rapporteur of Freedom of Religion and Belief (FoRB), who at that time was Heiner Bielefeldt. Behind the scenes working to make the forum a success was Chiew Yew Lin, FoRB's anchor, for without her, Heiner's visionary mission would not have been so meticulously implemented. This forum addressed the intersectional issues of two UN mandates—individual religious liberties and their impact on LGBTQ+ folks. The 150 attendees were made up of civil society organizations, religious leaders, scholars of religion, and diplomats from many countries.

On one panel, we had a trans activist Joleen Mataele from Tonga, whose parents kicked her out, forcing her into prostitution to provide for herself, and, later, a daughter. She suffered tremendous mental anguish and violence as a result of the hateful preaching of homosexuality from the local churches. Mataele is one of those charismatic personalities that you could not help but be drawn to. Her presentation was moving; pin-drop silence filled the room, and we all felt her pain. After her presentation, one of the church leaders who was sitting in the room spoke to her privately, and apologized for their contribution to her suffering.

That one outcome was worth the effort of co-organizing such a forum and, for me, was an outcome that overshadowed everything else.

On another occasion at a UN panel, a Jordanian diplomat came up to me and inquired, "Ani, we like the work you do, but do you HAVE to promote LGBTQ+ rights? Why push this Western agenda?" I responded with, "Did you know that Muslim societies did not have laws that criminalized homo-sexuality before colonization? Did you know that the coloniz-ers partially justified their colonial intent in order to counter the 'homo-friendly' Muslim societies? It was the colonizers who introduced their puritanical version of Christianity to the Muslim world, and it is, therefore, you, the Muslim states, who are promoting puritanical Christianity." He was stumped and sheepishly bid goodbye with a "See you next time," which, of course, never happened.

Most Muslims don't even know their own history, and they have no clue what Islam really is. What they know is based on what their governments and religious authorities want them to know. This is no different than Americans being raised on Christopher Columbus "discovering" America, or "A land without a people for a people without a land" in justifying the creation of Israel on Palestinian land, or the fairytale that the Pilgrims and the Native Americans gregariously sat down for a meal marketed as the first Thanksgiving. We've all been lied to by our respective governments, school systems, and religious leaders, and that is how they prefer us: dumb and dumber.

My visibility as an advocate of LGBTQ+ rights at the UN spaces resulted in me receiving many invitations to closed-door strategic and policy discussions in Geneva, London, and South Africa, which included a series of meetings toward the founding of the Global Interfaith Network for People of All Sexes, Sexual Orientations, Gender Identities, and Expressions (GINN-SOGIE).

Being an affective advocate requires you to keep an eye on policies. Just like when I was 12 years old paying close attention to foreign policy by reading the Far Eastern Economic Review, as an adult I now read the Foreign Affairs magazine and am a member of the Council for Foreign Relations, a reputable think tank and policy institution. In my own capacity, given my grassroots experiences and an eye on policies, I am consulted by various entities from large corporations to the EU in identifying gaps in their ideas, and recommending alternative approaches to their strategies. That is my strength.

For instance, when ex-British Prime Minister Theresa May apologized for colonial laws that discriminated against homosexuals that "still cause tremendous human rights violations," I jumped at the opportunity to create a concept note for a panel discussion at the Human Rights Council in Geneva titled "Pre-colonial Societies on Gender and Sexuality: A Hindu, Muslim, and Indigenous Peoples' Perspective." I partnered with GINN-SOGIE, and the panel was sponsored by the Permanent Missions of Iceland and South Africa with the South African Ambassador Mxakato-Diseko as the keynote speaker. The good thing about partnering with GINN-SOGIE is that, because they are based in South Africa, organizations in the Global South tend to be well funded. And in order to feature diverse voices that would debunk myths about homophobic religions and to pin the human rights violations on colonial laws, funding is key.

The panelists highlighted perspectives from the likes of Imam Dr Ludovic-Mohammed Zahed, a French gay imam of Algerian heritage; Dr Yvette Abrahams, a Khoesan Indigenous spiritual leader from South Africa; Manisha Dhakal, a Hindu from Nepal; Dr Elizabeth Kerekere of the Maori Indigenous spirituality from New Zealand; and I chaired the panel. Collectively, we proved the inclusive nature of societies toward LGBTQ+ folks in Western pre-colonial times, and it was the most eye-opening panel I ever chaired. We compared attitudes of the Hindu majority populations of India, which was colonized by the British, versus that of Nepal, which was not colonized. It was evident how the Indian society, with its criminalization of homosexuality encoded into law by the British, was much more homophobic in character than its neighbor, proving our point vividly.

In this one panel, we debunked the inherent homophobic nature religions are often accused of by anti-theist atheists and secular institutions, including the UN. We then highlighted

Indigenous spiritual and religious teachings that were affirming of homosexuality and sexual diversity, and I ended the panel with a call to action—asking for the Commonwealth countries to do away with the harmful colonial law criminalizing homosexuality. Given the anti-colonial sentiment rampant in ex-colonies, including the US, you'd think this would be an effortless undertaking, but unfortunately many countries, especially Muslim-majority countries, have embraced colonial homophobia as an Islamic principle and, if anything, have doubled down on it.

During the premiership of Prime Minister Najib in Malaysia, the government used to put on plays promoting hate for homosexuals in government-run high schools, while preachers and religious teachers controlled by the government's religious authorities such as JAKIM, also spewed hate on religious radio and television shows, and, of course, at Friday prayers across the country. Generally speaking, Christians in Malaysia too are just as homophobic, and any alternative, inclusive versions of this subject matter are censored and banned. The book "Gay is OK" by a friend and Malaysian-American Christian pastor-author, Ngeo Boon Lin, is banned, and Muslim organizations such as Queer Lapis and the one that I co-founded, Komuniti Muslim Universal, do the work of producing LGBTQ+ affirming content in Malay in our effort to chip away at government-sanctioned homophobia.

In 2023, Prime Minister Anwar Ibrahim was a guest at the Council for Foreign Relations, at which I attended virtually. He was asked to comment on discriminatory LGBTQ+ laws framed in how it is statistically proven to be bad for business and for the Gross Domestic Product (GDP) of a nation. His response was, "The overwhelming majority of Malaysians don't support homosexuality," deflecting responsibility to the will of the people rather than the responsibility of the government to protect all its citizens. I felt like yelling back at him "Well, what do you bloody expect when the government itself is guilty of promoting anti-LGBTQ+ attitudes!"

My public response to the numerous injustices I see is one of diplomacy and level-headedness, but in my head, there's sometimes a lot of yelling going on!

LGBTQ+ issues have a way of uniting strange bedfellows. Somehow hardened oppositional camps can set aside their differences and become a united front against this marginalized group of human beings.

In 2013, while in Paris to attend a conference, I happened to witness thousands of marchers, and making up a substantial group were bearded men and conservatively dressed women in scarves, Orthodox Jews and Muslims protesting together against the proposed same-sex marriage legislation. Similarly, here in the U.S., despite marriage equality interpreted as a constitutional right, it is strange how some heterosexuals go through great lengths to chisel away at the rights of LGBTQ+ folks and same-sex couples through legal means. Somehow, they see the rights of LGBTQ+ folks as a deprivation of their own rights and happiness.

Over the years, by way of court cases, there have been many efforts to strip away the rights of LGBTQ+ individuals and their families. I'm sure you know of the cake maker who refused to bake a wedding cake for a same-sex couple, and there have been so many cases since then.

There was also the case of the Catholic adoption service in Philadelphia that excluded same-sex couples from adopting. Now, by law, institutions that receive federal government funding cannot discriminate against couples, and because the Catholic Social Services of the Archdiocese of Philadelphia (CSS) did, the city of Philadelphia accused CSS of discrimination and withheld funding. So in the court case Fulton vs. Philadelphia, CSS sued the city, and they won. In other words, as a religious organization it is legal to receive government funding and discriminate.

For the record, I believe same-sex or heterosexual parents who go through great lengths to conceive a child through in vitro fertilization (IVF) or the very arduous process of adopting a child make for great parents because this can only happen out of an intense desire to love a child. And yes, it should be named, there are individuals in government who would like to see the total ban of IVF for "religious" reasons.

It is these instances that law firms and large civil society organizations involved in court cases often come to MPV for support in the form of filing amicus briefs. And it is through the involvement of various amicus briefs over many years that I have come to intimately learn of the issues and arguments being made in the name of the Religious Freedom Restoration Act (RFRA).

RFRA was signed into law by President Clinton to protect religious minorities, and the case that started it all was when peyote, a hallucinogenic cactus, was deemed an illegal drug by the U.S. government while Native Americans used it as part of their sacred ceremonials. Over the years, the Christian Right has successfully used the court system to justify their discriminatory beliefs as a "religious right" protected by RFRA. Although RFRA started off with the best of intentions of protecting religious minority rights, it is now being abused to discriminate in the name of religion, causing great harm.

The American Constitution primarily protects men, and on many occasions, laws have been passed to protect civil rights for the rest of us in bits and pieces, with exemptions for religious institutions. Yes, no one is allowed to discriminate against a fellow American, but if you belong to a religious institution, you can. Again, utterly appalling and despicable, and no wonder the youth have quit religion with 30 per cent of Americans now considering themselves "nones", those who no longer believe in a religious faith or tradition.

An example of the gaps in civil rights for non-straight men was when, in President Trump's first term, he allowed medical providers to withhold services to LGBTQ+ folks and abortion based on religious beliefs, which prompted critical questions about the intersection of law, religion, and discrimination. This again highlights the similarities between Sharia law and the laws legislated by the Christian Right, and the Supreme Court judges who adjudicate in their favor. The funny thing is, the very people who promoted a fake "creepin' sharia law" narrative against Muslims in America are the very people who are undermining the Constitution. As the Christian Right manipulates the court system to shield discriminatory beliefs under the guise of religious freedom, the separation of church and state is just a faint line in the sand, awash by numerous decisions of the Supreme Court in favor of those who brought these religious discriminatory cases to the fore. The legislation of their version of Christianity for everyone else has turned America into a theocracy.

I won't go into all the laws and cases argued under RFRA, as that would be volumes of books in itself, but as a human rights advocate, I know what theocracy looks like. Whether it be Saudi Arabia, Iran, or Israel, theocracies are failed states. We cannot allow America to go down that route any further.

Amidst the evolving Trump landscape, conservative Muslims have borrowed a page from the playbook of the Christian Right, deploying similar strategies for their own causes. In 2023, supported and funded by the Council of American-Islamic Relations (CAIR), conservative Muslims spearheaded protests against inclusive public school curricula, extending their campaign into Canada. In Montgomery, Maryland, Muslim parents were bused in from local mosques by CAIR's underlings, protesting at the Montgomery County Public School headquarters over the district's no-opt-out policy concerning LGBTQ+ inclusive storybooks.

To utilize RFRA, three Muslim families sued in a Montgomery, Maryland court, seeking their right to opt their children out of the inclusive public-school curriculum featuring images of same-sex parents, as well as a Muslim girl in hijab dancing. These inclusive curricula in Maryland, as well as in Detroit and

Los Angeles, strategically include various demographics of our multicultural and multi-religious communities, and part of the reason for doing so is because of the many years of bullying endured by LGBTQ+ children, and those endured by Muslim children post 9/11. Despite CAIR's many years of advocating against the bullying of Muslim kids, they demonstrated a double standard by overlooking the bullying of LGBTQ+ children. And therein lies the hypocrisy. Why can't we all work together against bullying of children regardless of who they are?

The case in Maryland argued that not allowing the Muslim parents to opt out of the inclusive curriculum impeded on their right to practice their religion. This is, of course, such a stretch, and the judge adjudicated against their claim. In public statements at a mosque gathering in Gaithersburg, Maryland, CAIR stated its intention to take this "All the way to the Supreme Court," foreseeing financial gains in the process. And sure enough, on April 22, 2025, the Supreme Court heard the case Tamer Mahmoud vs. Thomas W. Taylor.

Parallel to this havoc, more than 150 Muslim religious leaders, mostly from America and some from Canada, who previously claimed support of LGBTQ+ rights made a 180-degree turn and published their homophobic stance in a position statement titled "Navigating Differences." This document defended the right to discriminate against homosexuality while asserting protection against discrimination for its endorsers.

Realizing an opportunity, courting the Muslim Right in Detroit was General Michael Flynn, the election denier, and a rabid Islamophobe. As of July 2023, he's an ex-Islamophobe and in a two-hour-long conversation recorded on video, we see him making a sales pitch seeking partnership with Hamtramck's Muslim mayor, religious and community leaders about how "We need to set our differences aside and work together on our shared values." The shared values are their "family values," which is code for anti-LGBTQ+ and against wokeism.

There is circumstantial evidence that correlates with the increased number of Muslims who voted for Trump the second time around, and why? In unofficial and unscientific data, informal interviews conducted by an ally Imam reveal that mosque-going Muslims don't care for the "LGBTQ+ agenda" and for "Black Lives Matter."

In the 2024 elections, more Muslims voted for Trump due to the crisis in Gaza and Lebanon, and the early courtship of the mayor of Hamtramck by Flynn paid off with the mayor endorsing Trump.

Instead of advancing LGBTQ+ rights, in the US, there is a coordinated effort to erode these rights through the passage of numerous state legislations. Challenges at the state level will inevitably go all the way up to the Supreme Court, and with the number of conservative judges dominating the Supreme Court—just like Talibans in their robes, we have seen cases adjudicated to the detriment of women's reproductive rights, LGBTQ+ rights in healthcare, and voting rights, to name a few, relegating these victims as second-class citizens.

To protect American citizens regardless of sex, the Equal Rights Amendment (ERA), is an effort to ratify the 28th Constitutional Amendment. It was proposed 100 years ago in Seneca Falls,

July 20, 1923, by Alice Paul. To commemorate the 100th year anniversary, I spoke at the very podium Alice Paul spoke. As Americans, regardless of whether you're Muslim, non-Muslim, or non-faith—we should all be championing this constitutional amendment, which will finally give all American citizens equal status under the law. Having met the requirements for a constitutional amendment, it is technically the law of the land, but given how, under the second Trump administration, laws have been upended, we find ourselves fighting for civil rights we thought we had already won.

Unless you are directly impacted by Supreme Court decisions, most Americans don't pay enough attention to this very important branch of government. And they absolutely should. Fortunately, there are organizations such as Lambda Legal and private large law firms that volunteer in defending cases pro bono, protecting our collective rights while defending us against the American Talibans in suits and religious robes.

While this is being played out domestically, the organization Ipas reveals there has been an alliance between Family Watch International, a Christian Right entity, and the 57-Muslim member Organization of Islamic Cooperation (OIC) at the international level. The OIC has rolled out its strategy of pushing back against the "LGBTQ+ agenda" with "family values" at their respective country level and at the UN. It is unfortunate that the OIC is still steeped in its colonial mindset, finding familiarity and solace in this new 21st century Christian colonizer.

For LGBTQ+ and Black folks and the progressive Left who have stood up for the rights of Muslims, who protested against the

Muslim ban in New York at the historic Stonewall Inn, who helped paint over walls of mosques spewed with messages of hate from White Supremacists, who have invited imams and religious leaders into their churches in brotherly and sisterly love, we have come back full circle to 2008, when the Shura Council in Southern California mobilized their constituencies to ban marriage equality. The current scenario echoes the divisive actions of 2008, which show the cyclical nature of these challenges and underscore the importance of the ongoing struggle for understanding, and the importance of allyship in our collective struggle to lift everyone up together, and leave no one behind.

\*\*\*

# 12
# What is an American Muslim culture?

In his "Remaining Awake Through a Great Revolution" address, Dr Martin Luther King Jr. made the poignant observation about Sunday being the most segregated day of the week. I realized that Dr King's truth applied to Muslims too.

It is not just a Christian thing, but Muslims too, have their segregated places of worship. Mosques in America, for the most part, are segregated not only along denominational but also along ethnic lines. There are the Thai, the Somali, the Persian/Iranian, the African American, etc. mosques.

It is human nature to want to be around "your tribe," but that mindset has never appealed to me. I understand the gravitational pull, the comfort of being surrounded by the same mindset and same culture, like running and fasting with my buddies during Ramadan. But I also crave the diversity I had grown up with, and it became part of my ethos to continue to learn from people who are not like me.

Despite the segregated mosques, the one thing that has unified American Muslims is the shift toward the values espoused in Wahhabism. Regardless of denomination or ethnicity, these teachings have become a common thread narrowingly defining a "good" Muslim. This theology forces Muslims into a small box they exclusively labeled "Islam" when in my opinion, Islam was revealed to liberate humanity from being boxed in. The Quran spoke against allegiance to tribal ways, to a monarch, patriarchy, and even to God itself, declaring "there is no compulsion in faith."

Instead of prioritizing freedom of thought and intellectual prowess, truthfulness, and character, what is insisted upon is external mores—if you're a woman, it is compulsory to wear a hijab; and if you're a man, you are to wear a beard. For many decades, this uniformity was promoted in America by conservative Muslim organizations, which I wrote about earlier.

It should be noted that the only mention of the term *hijab* in the Quran is that of a wooden screen. Prophet Muhammad's home was also a community space; as such, there was no privacy for his family members. Members of the community were therefore advised to speak to his family and wife through the *hijab,* a wooden screen.

On the matter of modesty, the Quran advises women to draw your shawl over your bosom. Just like today, in the 700s, women were judged by their attire. (Yes, it is sad how we have not evolved much!) Slaves went bare-chested, and the higher the class, the more you were allowed to cover yourself. If you were of a lower class and covered up to resemble that of a higher class, you would be publicly whipped. That was the classist and tribal system of the day. By stating women should cover their bosom, the Quran was leveling the classist system. The best book on this subject matter is "The Veil and the Male Elite" by Fatima Mernissi.

And that is why I don't wear a *hijab*.

Engaging in interfaith activities in post-9/11 Los Angeles unveiled the fractures and the superficiality of some of these interfaith collaborations. I remember one instance while standing in line at a buffet dinner, I struck up a conversation with a woman behind me. As per the tradition at these interfaith gatherings, we introduced ourselves and the faith tradition that we belong to. As if she was a Wahhabist herself, with her head cocked backward and eyes squinting, this Christian woman asked, "Then, why are you not wearing a headscarf?"

Around the same time, I was invited to do the call for prayer at an interfaith Thanksgiving dinner in Los Angeles. Upon learning of my invitation, instead of supporting me, the imams of the interfaith group warned the organizing committee that they would not attend and would discourage their congregation from attending if I, a woman, was to do the call for prayer. This blatant exclusionary attitude signaled a troubling trend within these interfaith alliances.

These types of arm-twisting stances have been rampant within many interfaith groupings, and I don't see the progressive churches and synagogues pushing back against the exclusionary attitudes of the conservative Muslims. As a result, over the years, with few exceptions, I have abandoned these interfaith circles unless I can show up as myself.

In running MPV for over 18 years, I have had the privilege of seeing various cultural practices within the Muslim communities from the prism of those who have chosen to leave their particular communities for ours. How it is practiced, its traditions, dogma, and beliefs is very much rooted in the cultural tradition of a particular country and/or *mazhab* or denomination. The richness of these traditions is vast. In other words, our American Muslim identity is a plurality of traditions that depends on which country you immigrated from, or, for African American Muslims, from which tradition they have chosen to adopt for themselves.

The American Muslims of Pakistani heritage have their distinctive culture and, for some, not all, have a deep Sufi spiritual path with rich poetry and music such as that of Fatih Ali Khan. This very brief description doesn't do the subject matter justice, as this is a book unto itself, but it is important to understand the context of the diversity within the Muslim community in America.

Due to the diversity of traditions, the plurality of languages and values, the cultures that express Muslim traditions are also rich. But many of the people from these rich traditions have not been accepting of a new communal, progressive American Islam—one that reflects an egalitarian and inclusive interpretation and expression of its faith. For example, in a traditional mosque, the imam leading gender-segregated prayer spaces will always be a man, while in the progressive Muslim community we often have a female imam leading a coed congregation in prayer, in an unsegregated space, where families can pray together, and where LGBTQ+ folks

are welcome. This inclusive American Muslim religious culture was stamped by a landmark Friday prayer service by Dr
amina wadud in New York City in 2005, followed by a bur-
geoning culture that I have helped shape since 2006. ("amina
wadud" is spelled in lower case as that is her preference.)

Although the Quran does not prohibit Muslims from praying
in their mother tongue, our ritual prayers are usually in Arabic,
and depending on who is leading the prayer, each Arabic
phrase will be followed with an English translation. One such
woman imam communal prayer, viewed over 2.6 million times,
is available on MPV's YouTube channel, and looking at the
comments, many have clearly not liberated themselves from
their patriarchal mindsets, nor are they interested in reading
the theological validation for such a prayer service.

Praying in Arabic would be equivalent to Christians praying
in Aramaic or Catholics in Latin. For many American Muslims,
when reciting the Quran in Arabic, most don't know what
they are reciting verbatim, some only get the gist of what they
are reciting. This is why at MPV we make sure to educate the
meaning of the verses of the Quran.

One aspect of our American Muslim religious-cultural practices is gender segregation in mosques. This Wahhabist practice was one of the first things we at MPV chose to eliminate.
Women in Wahhabi mosques are relegated to separate prayer
spaces, sometimes hidden behind walls, perpetuating a rigid
hierarchy. Although Saudi Arabia is changing its stance now,
Wahhabism for the past 70 years has been at the forefront
of extreme segregation of the sexes, usually not just a wall

that separates the sexes in the prayer halls, but sometimes a completely different room in the mosque where the women cannot even see the *imam* but only hear him through a set of speakers. For vivid examples of women's prayer spaces, check out Hind Makki's "@SideEntrance" on X.

Following the conversations on @SideEntrance, there is a running joke among some of the women who attend these severely segregated mosques—that their favorite mosque events are interfaith ones, where they get to share the same luxurious space as the men. One example was on International Refugee Day when Angelina Jolie, as ambassador to the United Nations High Commissioner for Refugees, was a guest speaker at a mosque in Washington, D.C. She spoke at the podium where no other Muslim woman would have been allowed, and she wore a long skirt reaching just below her knees, which no Muslim woman would have been allowed to wear in a mosque.

In some cases, segregation is also enforced in social settings such as meals and lecture halls, and women have to enter the mosque through the back door, while of course, men enter through the front.

At the Grand Mosque in Indonesia, the largest Muslim country, men and women have open prayer spaces, women on one side, men on the other, and they all enter through the same grand entrances. As a guest of the Grand Imam of Indonesia, Nasaruddin Umar and his staff were generous with their time to take me on a tour of the mosque complex. I was without a hijab, and we walked into the prayer areas, onto the carpet and into the men's section. Nobody freaked out!

In America, in mosques that adhere to Wahhabi practices, which comprise the majority of mosques in the US, men and women don't usually greet each other with a handshake, and the way you wear the *hijab* better not reveal a strand of hair, or someone will tell you off. Women, no matter how educated in Islam, are never to lead a coed congregation in prayer, because according to a *hadith*, *"the soul of a woman is lesser than that of a man,"* and *"God will not accept your prayer should you pray behind a woman."* This is, of course, a bastardization of Islam, patriarchy on steroids. And just as a reminder, the hadith are writings of men from the medieval period.

In the spring of 2024, I received the cutest letter from a second grader. She wrote: "My name is Yasmine and I am seven years old. My father is a Muslim. I want to address the matter that women and men do not get to pray together in mosques. Women cannot pray with their families and they feel left out. This might make some women not want to participate. As a young person, I do not understand why men and women are treated unequally. I think this is really unfair. Please consider the idea I have shared and think about possibly making changes…We should not be separated. When praying with our families, we're better together."

I love the fact that even this seven-year-old could see the misogyny, and tells me to do something about it! Yasmine and I are now pen pals!

So here's the beautiful truth we were never taught. The first female *imam*, Um Waraqah, was appointed by Prophet Muhammad himself, and she led men and women in prayer.

He also appointed the first woman to manage the head of religious studies and the first woman to head the social service department when he governed the secular state of Medina. Yet, lo and behold, in the 21st century, women's voices have been sexualized and deemed as sexually enticing, which is why women are prohibited from teaching adult men, and that is also why we predominantly hear Quran recitations by men only.

This starkly contrasts with my upbringing. When my father chaired the International Quran Reading Competition in Malaysia, the women's category included audiences that were—and continue to be—of mixed gender, meaning men listening to female reciters. It was this exposure growing up, the normalization of a women's voice in reciting the Quran and in Islamic spiritual songs, or *nasyeed/nashid*, that made me averse to the Wahhabi version of Islam that dominates much of the world.

In America, music, and even wishing others Christmas or Hanukkah greetings, have become *haram*, forbidden. Every year, on social media, I see posts by young Muslims asking their religious leaders the permissibility of greeting their non-Muslim neighbors and colleagues. Greeting someone on their traditional holiday meant showing respect and acknowledgment. During Prophet Muhammad's time, when the wake of a Jewish man passed by in the street, he stood up to show respect. One cannot imagine a deeper expression of dignityand humanity. Our Islamic culture is filled with such examples—but unfortunately, that is not what many of our modern-day religious leaders preach or teach.

The majority of the Muslim world, including here in America, talks a good talk about how ahead of its time Islam was in advancing women's rights. This is absolutely true, but they certainly don't live by it. Their teachings not only omit the revolutionary appointments Prophet Muhammad gave to women in Medina, but also the secular manner in which he governed over the non-Muslim tribes, the many covenants he made with Jewish and Christian tribes to protect them, his kindness toward children, and his care for animals and the environment.

Culture is influenced by religion.When the religion that is taught is misogynistic, homophobic, and dogmatic, the culture of that society will also be imbued with those values. Culture, to many people—especially policymakers and funders—isn't taken seriously enough. They keep funding the same secular human rights framing, which do not resonate with the very constituencies whose cultures they are trying to change.

***

So now we know that the current American Muslim culture is not homegrown American, but that of the cultures from which we came from.

With hundreds of mixed-faith couples married, many are struggling to find a safe space for them to raise their children in an inclusive Muslim community. Just like the negative experiences my daughter had at her Islamic Sunday School, many of the couples I've married share the same unfortunate experiences, and ones they do not wish for their children.

Toward creating an American Muslim faith tradition that is rooted in universal values, along with early-child-development expert, Shaleena Tareen, I co-authored the Inclusive Islam Curriculum. Our curriculum focuses on values of the Quran, weaving in the different faith traditions with the same set of values, constructing an inclusive worldview from a young age. We promote respect and love for all of God's creations—the diversity of humankind, the animal kingdom, and the environment. The curriculum emphasizes the importance of critical thinking and the freedom to express oneself, the importance of philanthropy, nurturing the child's identity into one of confidence and for a purposeful life, and we do this through various artistic expressions and songs; songs that I have written, produced, and sung.

Just as I was raised through a prism of non-discrimination, of multiculturalism, and of multi-faith, children should be imbued with these values from a young age. We shouldn't be teaching children that our faith is the only right path and everyone else is condemned to hell. We should be teaching children the universality of our collective spirituality and that we are all God's children. The Sanskrit term *Namaste,* which means "the spirit in me sees the spirit in you," encapsulates the humanity of each one of us beautifully.

Children are never too young to learn about charity or *zakat;* if anything, they should be taught to research which charities reflect their values, and ways of supporting those charities. Children should also be taught how to think critically and be encouraged to think for themselves, how to build justification for their position, and, most importantly, to express them respectfully. These lessons are designed to appeal to the intellect and the heart, quite different from how most children are taught, that is, the memorizing of sacred texts with no explanation of what they mean.

*** 

"God is closer to you than your jugular vein," states the Quran. And Prophet Muhammad was known to have said in the hadith, "to know yourself is to know God."

Our Creator is the most creative entity, as evident in the diversity of plants, animals, humankind, and the universe. It is written in the Quran that around 120 days of pregnancy, God blows its spirit into the womb. In Christianity, this is termed ensoulment. By default, with this spirit we too are creative. It is what makes us human, different from the rest of the animal kingdom. Therefore, to censor our creativity is to kill our creative spirit, our connection to the God in us. With that, it hardens our heart, and in Islamic Sufi tradition, a hardened heart is one without empathy. It is what makes us cruel to oneself and to others.

Many in our progressive community love music, and I believe the absence of music is like missing a part of life. The idea that music is *haram,* as claimed by conservative Muslims, is a way to unhinge our spiritual connection with the Creator—with the God in us.

Unlike the spiritual musical expressions that existed for centuries in Muslim societies, spiritual music as a form of worship is prohibited in the Sunni Islam tradition in America. Contrast that to the rich, spiritual, worshiping songs in gospel music and church choirs, which I find enormously uplifting and moving. Evangelical churches always have music. While traveling in Africa, you can tell an Evangelical church by the music genre, which draws in the youth and fills everyone's hearts. Music is spiritual.

Can you imagine going to church and not singing "Oh Come, All Ye Faithful" or a Christmas service without singing "Gloria in Excelsis Deo"? I can't. It's why I love my Christmas service at All Saints Church Pasadena.

Unlike these Christian traditions, without this music element American Muslims are not building an emotional memory that connects us to faith. There is science behind the concept of emotional memory. It is that emotion you feel when you hear a particular song that reminds you of a particular event or moment in your life. Till today, I get teary eyed when I hear Louis Armstrong's "What a Wonderful World." I can picture my father singing, in his white singlet and sarong on Sundays. Or when I hear a Led Zeppelin song, I hear and see my late brother Aza rocking it. I smile, and I cry.

This emotional memory is uniquely human, and the science should be utilized to create a spiritual and positive emotional memory with Islam.

That is why I believe creating an American Muslim music tradition will go far in transforming our collective hearts, reconnecting us to the God in us, to love, and to compassion, regardless of what version of Islam you practice or one's cultural heritage.

To that end, I've spent the last 17 years creating, writing, and producing songs for a new genre called "Islamic Hymns". This is a body of musical works that can be used as worship songs in English. The first album "Ummah Wake Up" were songs that promoted social justice issues with titles such as "Just Like Khadija," which is about Prophet Muhammad's first wife, the businesswoman who financed the survival of the early Muslim community. In the song "Just Like Khadija" I wrote and sang:

"Just like Khadija, I want to be strong

Stand up for what's rights and fight what's wrong

Just like Khadija, I want to be that girl

A super Muslim woman in this world"

In "Bury Me" I sing about female infanticide:

"I am Allah's creation, I don't deserve discrimination

Controlling and honor killing; There's no room for that the Quran says"

The second project is titled "One", an acoustic collection that included interfaith-themed songs, such as a collaboration with Rabbi Naomi Levy titled "Oneness of God." The third project is "Islamic Hymns—Celebration of Life," where I return to my classical music roots with strings and choral vocal arrangements, and lyrics by Rumi, Rabia al-Basri, and verses from the Quran.

This body of work is my way of defying the prohibition of female singing voices, and of music in general while utilizing the spirituality of music for an Islam in the West. I hope that one day someone will take some of these songs toward creating an American Muslim choir, one that will perform side by side with the Baptist Church Choir, the Tabernacle Choir, and the Gay Men's Chorus at the National Mall in Washington, D.C., in celebration of July 4th. When that moment happens, American Muslims will finally be included in the fabric of America.

The development of an American Muslim culture is a necessary next step. There has always been a unique Muslim culture in many parts of the Muslim world. There are numerous and varying Arab and African Muslim traditions, just as there are Chinese and Malay ones. Despite what many would proclaim, an American Muslim culture would not be blasphemous.

Over the years, I have strived to cultivate a culture that transcends the divisive values propagated by misogynistic, homophobic, and dogmatic teachings. By returning to the roots of Quranic teachings of justice and by shedding unjust and harmful cultural practices, the end result is to embody the essence of spiritual equality—where men, women, and all genders stand as equals, in liberty and justice for all.

By creating the curriculum, the egalitarian spiritual practices and prayer spaces, and the body of spiritual music, I believe I have created the building blocks for an American Islam cultural tradition that is rooted in universal values, where everyone regardless of gender, sexual orientation, ethnicity or race, is truly equal. This is what I have given back to my adopted country.

# 13
# The politics of human rights

Through my years of human rights work, the energy that drives me is anger. Anger against the inhumane way large swaths of populations are treated and oppressed, some based on race, gender, and sexual identity, and many justified in the name of religion. We know in anger we have uttered awful things that have gotten us in trouble and can be a destructive energy. Anger can also be an endless source of constructive energy.

The omission of the full truth by religious leaders in justifying prejudices and the promotion of hate of "the other" is despicable. Despicable, too, are those, mostly Western democracies, who tout a feminist foreign policy while claiming to uphold human rights values, only to bare their naked prejudices in whose human life they really value. As a reminder, just because one is a female leader, it does not necessarily make one a feminist in its purest definition that lifts everyone up, not just women.

Vice President Kamala Harris and the Democratic Party gatekeepers denying an American Palestinian the opportunity to speak at the Democratic Convention in 2024 illustrated the hypocrisy of the "inclusive" policy she was touting. The American

Israeli parents and hostage Hersh Goldberg-Polin were kinder in acknowledging the thousands of dead Palestinians at the podium of the Democratic Convention. It was remarkable how tone-deaf Harris and her team were. Literally, all they had to do was listen to the roar and the lengthy applause whenever Gaza was mentioned by other presenters. And if emotion didn't count, then they could have studied data indicating the overwhelming majority of the Democratic constituency, the youth, the LGBTQ+ community, Independents and especially the American Jewry who supported a ceasefire.

For my part, while sitting at home in Los Angeles, I feverishly reached out to contacts I knew who could have swayed Kamala in including a vetted Palestinian speaker with a vetted speech, and thus avoided her from making a colossal mistake. I texted Minnesota's Attorney General Keith Ellison. Since Tim Waltz is Governor, surely Keith could just text him. Sadly, his response was "Sorry Ani, I haven't been able to reach Tim since he has been tapped as VP."

The next person I reached out to is a rabbi friend who is also Hersh Goldberg-Polin's uncle. I texted the rabbi, "I know this is a difficult ask, but do you think Hersh's parents could talk to Kamala's team about allowing a Palestinian to speak at the podium?" The rabbi declined given the emotional toll Hersh's parents were already enduring.

Yes, calling for a ceasefire—the mass killing of innocent people, especially that of children is somehow political. And with that radar-less moral compass, the support for Kamala dissipated. A large number of American voters were too disgusted, and they were willing to see Trump burn the country down as mapped out in Project 2025. Within two months into Trump's presidency, he is doing just that, and with a breathtaking level of corruption.

Throughout my life, as I've shared, there have been nuggets of beautiful experiences that have come from connecting with fellow human beings, both negative and positive. Even negative ones result in a thin silver lining, which has challenged me to do better, think differently, or approach the problem creatively. In order to see and benefit from a silver lining, you have to be open-hearted, surrender to the process, seize what's before you. The key lies not merely in observing but in embracing the moment when the opportunity unveils itself. It's about detaching from the cacophony of the noise outside and delving into the inner spirit. Kamala Harris failed to tap into her powerful inner spirit and instead surrendered to corrupt lobbyists.

Sexism, racism, and patriarchy are values based on ego. Regardless of gender, they are deeply entrenched in us as humans. Many social justice movements utilize the same egoistic values to undo injustice, and that doesn't work as it only entrenches "the other." The "cancel" culture is another form of oppression. It encourages censorship and erasure of "others" when what we need is dialogue.

For example, taking the position of eliminating the State of Israel to bring long-overdue justice for a Palestinian State doesn't work, as does the long-ignored Israeli occupation and its documented intention, its genocide of the Palestinian people, their culture, and their aspirations.

Unfortunately, what I just expressed results in vile attacks and being canceled. I understand that sometimes one has to express themselves in extreme ways to be heard, but it ends up delegitimizing a justified cause. In these times, a positive voice is drowned out by a tsunami of negative storylines and headlines, because the financial gains from hate and clicks supersede that of justice and understanding. Each one of us can do our part by refraining from clicking and sharing hate.

As a way to amplify our anti-hate advocacy, in 2018, MPV secured Consultative Status, which gives us more access to the UN system. With that status we championed against the hate of religious minority rights in Muslim-majority countries, the rights of ex-Muslims, and we highlighted the work of progressive Muslims all over the world. We submitted this input to the Special Rapporteur for freedom of religion and belief at the time, Ahmed Shaheed, and it has taken us many reports and different UN channels to make our narrative heard and relevant, not just to UN agencies but to Western democracies that read the reports, some adjusting their domestic and foreign policies accordingly.

After many years of speaking up for the rights of minorities, and being strategically vocal in highlighting the hate and threats directed at progressive Muslims from conservative and radical Muslims, it was rewarding to be commissioned by the United Nations Office on Genocide Prevention and the Responsibility to Protect to create an anti-hate-speech workshop for Muslim-majority communities. This commissioning came at a time when Pakistani Christians and Shias were violently and unjustly persecuted not only by vigilantes but also by the judicial system, an injustice that is ongoing. Once I was done with designing the workshop, I was ready to implement it, but of course, that's when I hit the wall. Funding for the roll-out got pulled.

The politics of human rights is intertwined with money. The hard work of advancing it is rife with hurdles, the path loaded with landmines.

Although stringent definitions of what is prescribed as hate speech are well established, policies to combat differ or are void depending on which community or group that hate speech is directed at. Replace any hate speech directed at Muslims with "Jews," "Blacks" or "gays," and you will get a different government response from the American and most European governments, despite having signed on to numerous treaties on this issue. Muslim-majority governments are not as hypocritical because at least they don't pretend to uphold and defend human rights values!

While international frameworks exist, their implementation remains a challenge. Progress in this realm requires a collective effort to dismantle discriminatory ideologies, especially within our own respective communities. And this requires tremendous courage.

Look at how Jews who have spoken up against Israel's genocide of the Palestinian people are vilified not just by members of their own families and communities, but even American legislators have passed bills to ban speech that the government deems as supporting "terrorism."

Fighting injustice perpetrated by your own community is really hard. I've had my share of threats, and ostracization.

Now, if I am to identify as an ex-Muslim and demonize Islam, or a pro-Zionist Muslim, I would be rolling in money, publishing offers up the gazoo, and opportunities to speak at large and secular platforms. There are many names I could list who have benefited in this manner, but I won't. Although I am self-critical of Muslims and many of the Muslim religious authorities, I am still Muslim, and I choose to utilize the rights-affirming progressive Islam in challenging patriarchy, racism, and sexism... and surprise, surprise, that's not what the powers want to hear.

Non-Muslims who cheer me on for challenging human rights violations in the name of Islam relish the critique, but when I apply the same human rights standards to their communities, as in the case of Israel, then I am deemed prejudiced or racist.

Armed with sacred texts, Muslims in Muslim societies also criticize human rights violations particularly those in the hands of their governments. It is also for these reasons that many Muslims are jailed, tortured, or killed for advocating for a just system in their countries. Sometimes governments don't have to silence outspoken human rights defenders, vigilantes will do the deed for them. But how can an individual be so angered and riled up as to justify murder? How can the murder of a Christian Nigerian young woman, Deborah Samuel Yakubu, by a vigilante Muslim mob for blasphemy be justified?

The answer lies in how politicians and religious authorities shape the mindsets of their constituencies. It starts young.

Just like the conversation I had with the young man in Tunisia, the information religious authorities omit such as the right to leave Islam, and that there is no punishment for apostasy or blasphemy. Prophet Muhammad certainly didn't punish anyone for insulting him, and yet some Muslims feel they have the right to murder another for "insulting" Islam and the Prophet.

Prophet Muhammad and Islam do not need defending.

It is important to pay attention and to challenge the information we consume, and sometimes more importantly, the omission of information. A long time ago, a journalist friend advised me when reading the news to read in between the lines, pay attention to what is insinuated and what is not said.

The policy briefs produced for the "Global Exchange on Religion in Society" conference in Brussels in 2019, in which statistics depicting American Muslims as overwhelmingly progressive were omitted, is one example (Grifth-Dickson et al., 2019).

The omission of parts of these facts is a disservice to the public and to policymakers but it is designed to ensure Muslims are still viewed as the dangerous ilk, stubborn in their archaic religious values, and foreign to "the Western egalitarian and human rights values." The omission of any information, whether it be in media or in religion, is to misinform the target audience, to shape their mindsets in a biased manner. My experiences with the bias in reporting in regards to the exchange I had with Ilhan Omar and the publication of "Navigating Differences," which omitted the description of sexual diversity in the Quran, are just a few examples of many.

Of course, it doesn't help when supposed liberals like the television host Bill Maher, a rabid anti-theist atheist with a particular interest in denigrating Islam, are influencers in their own right. I watch Bill Maher religiously. Sorry for the pun! But Bill has no clue what Islam is about and has adopted its radical version as "truth." It makes the work of undermining patriarchal Islam so much harder. When it comes to Islam he is intellectually dishonest, and it's a cop-out because he's not dumb. Having Bill talk about Islam would be equivalent to me talking about marijuana. To me, marijuana leaves are all green so they must all be the same. See how stupid of an assessment that is? Similarly, Bill Maher's assessment of Islam is just as stupid.

Like I said earlier, the human rights double standards and how they reveal one's prejudice bare naked for the world to see in how Russia's war on Ukraine was treated compared to that of Israel's war on the Palestinian people.

The EU touts with pride their feminist foreign policy, well, being a feminist means justice and equality for women and for society at large. The bombing of Ukrainian hospitals and civilian infrastructure by Russia was swiftly condemned by the European Commission President Ursula von der Leyen as a war crime, while silent of Israel's destruction of 18 hospitals (and counting), the complete destruction of water-purifying plants, schools, universities, cultural centers, the equestrian center and its horses, and the targeting of civilians with white phosphorus, which are all war crimes. And for that double standard, von der Leyen was called out by some members of the EU. It is again evident that just because one is a female political leader does not mean one is a feminist, nor can we automatically assume she will be a more compassionate and just leader.

In another example of the politics of human rights, in a letter to the Human Rights Council, the European Union called out China's treatment of the Uighurs as genocide. The Uighurs are a Chinese Muslim population, imprisoned en masse, the children separated from their parents and "re-educated" of their culture in what the UN terms "cultural genocide." The adults are used as forced labor for many clothing brands in the Western market, which you probably unknowingly purchased.

Meanwhile, in reference to the Uighurs, the Organization of Islamic Cooperation submitted a letter to the Human Rights Council commending China for its handling of "terrorists," disagreeing with the UN's classification that China is conducting a cultural genocide.

The politics of human rights can give you a whiplash. To claim you stand for universal human rights values only when it is convenient is not only unprincipled, but hypocritical.

My refugee immigration lawyer friend el-Farouk Khaki in Toronto co-wrote an op-ed berating the unfair system in Canada where special privileges were created that benefited only Ukrainian refugees giving them visas and work permits (Khaki and Aidan, 2022). Contrast that with refugees from Gaza, which were limited in nature and halted for "security concerns." Somehow, it has escaped the Trudeau government that its military support of Israel has contributed to a surge in Palestinian refugees.

The US too is full of contradictions. It promotes itself as the torchbearer of human rights, but again only when it is convenient. It is revolting. As of December 2024, President Biden is complicit in arming Israel as it stands accused of genocide at the International Court of Justice, a UN court system that upholds international agreements, and in this case, the Genocide Convention, which was drawn up soon after the Holocaust so that we may "never again" see the annihilation of a people.

The cheapest American-made bomb, a "dumb" bomb, can cost up to a few thousand dollars. The amount of destruction caused by this dumb bomb is an example of a dumb philosophy of war. Imagine what positive outcomes could come from feeding and caring for people rather than destroying lives. Besides destruction, the trauma of war—whether as a victim or the killer—is not easy to overcome.

For $5,000, the approximate cost of a dumb bomb, I can implement a yearlong #TeenClub program at a coed Muslim high school of 1,500 teenagers. I can teach them about critical thinking, human rights, peaceful reconciliation, and positive masculinity to both sexes so that they can learn how to treat each other with respect. This reduces future cases of domestic violence, unexpected pregnancies, and, for young women, it is important for them to recognize a positive masculine man when they are ready to choose a partner.

All this hypocrisy in religion, foreign policy, and human rights enrages me, especially when I have observed the manipulation that is taking place behind the scenes. But

I also know that underneath the miserable headlines are the many good works and positive efforts by people all over the world. Being in touch with many who do these good works allows me to see the world differently and positively. It brings me peace in my heart.

Seeing a young woman smile, stand up straight with dignity after a workshop I taught or spearheaded, or receiving messages of thanks from LGBTQ+ Muslims that the work we do has lifted them from depression or dissuaded them from attempting suicide is fulfilling. Or hearing from the many interfaith-wedded couples who have been able to tie the knot, enjoined by families of different faiths and traditions. All this comes from an anger to defy the patriarchy in the form of religious belief, and the politics of divide and conquer, of us against them, and the false societal structures of control. Patriarchy is the antithesis of self-determination, which is a prerequisite to happiness.

By challenging the patriarchy with alternative and gender-affirming narratives, I have created an ecosystem or nests from which people can flourish. It has helped many feel safe, giving them the tools to argue for their own right to self-determination and human dignity. Like a bird that has outgrown their nests, they need a sturdy tree branch to push themselves off to fly. I see myself as a tree branch. The unfortunate experience I've had is that, on many occasions, the birds shit on the tree branch before taking off, never to hear from them again. Sometimes though, it is the very same Muslim women and LGBT+ folks who shit on the very branch that nested them and helped them fly.

Marginalized people also have a tendency to harm those who help them. It is rooted in trauma. It hurts, but I get over it when I think that at least that bird is healed enough to be able to fly, and hopefully, it will live a purposeful life not just for itself but also give back to others.

After many layers of bird poop on my branch, my friends and board members at MPV expressed concern about me burning out. Personally, I don't understand the concept of "burning out." Of course, I've had plenty of ups and downs, but that fire in my belly rages through.

I remember some years ago when I was working every day and way beyond ten hours a day, which started to affect my family dynamics and the amount of time I spent with my loved ones. One night, I said a quiet prayer, "Good God! Please turn down that fire in my belly!" only to wake up to an even larger fire.

I never understood why I don't burn out until I heard a lecture by a mental health counselor at the Los Angeles County Department of Mental Health Liaison for the Faith-Based Advocacy Council (FBAC), who said, "For some of you, the work you do aligns with your values, and instead of burning you out, it replenishes your energy and reinforces your purpose in life."

And that's what it is, a purpose in life. My purpose in life.

I know I will probably never retire. There is still so much to do in life, and I will probably continue working in some capacity and keeping the commitments I made for myself till my deathbed.

Even as my father was ill after a heart attack in May of 1985, he put a Glyceryl Trinitrate pill (GTN) under his tongue to finish typing his last letter to me. With numerous heart attacks in the last years of his life at age 60, he was still aspiring to serve the public in his home state of Kedah.

Just like how he lived his life, I wish I could tell him now, "Look Dad, I made my life count too."

# Assignment suggestions

1.  Read Chapter 5, watch and critique "al-imam," a short film about Ani Zonneveld's work as an imam and advocacy for universal human rights, //voxpopulisphere.com/2018/12/16/video-al-imam/, and support your critique for or against the right for women imams or women in religious leadership roles (rabbis, pastors, priests).

2.  Read Chapter 3 and contemplate if there is anything in your life where you were forbidden from doing something because of your gender, or if you became consumed by fear, hindering you from doing what you want because of your gender.

3.  Read Chapter 5. Child and forced marriage is an issue in many countries. What makes child marriage in the US different from that in Afghanistan? Give a minimum of three points, similarities and/or differences.

4.  Read Chapter 7. If you were censored by social media companies and your freedom of speech silenced by your government, strategize the steps you would take in overcoming these challenges, and how you would SAFELY fight back.

5.  Israeli and Palestinian families bereave together in the organization The Parents Circle Families Forum, https://www.theparentscircle.org/en/homepage-en/. Study the group. Map out what ways they have succeeded and failed, and list how you would have organized differently.

# References

Al-imam. (2016). *Los Angeles: Omar Al-Dakheel, Director.* [Online] Vox Populi. Available at: https://wp.me/p4xqzG-8og

Ani/Zonneveld, Z. (2003). *Ummah Wake Up.* Available at: open.spotify.com/artist/09l3WDq7qTgDWByX3kYYIL?si=LcMmxZcb RfyjquivPTMqvg

Grifth-Dickson, G., Hussain, D., Mandaville, P., Dickson, A., Farrag, S., Mian, M., Siddiqi, N. and Smith, J. (2019). The Lokahi Foundation. *Islam, Diversity & Context*, pp. 24-25. Available at: www.academia.edu/39905990/ISLAM_DIVERSITY_and_CONTEXT

Isaac, R. M. (2023). *Sermon in the Liturgy of Lament: Christ in the Rubble.* Available at: https://youtu.be/aEGiANa0-ol?si=_LqFpj7il4DxepWc

Keb'Mo/Moore, K and Zonneveld, Z. (2014). *One Friend.* [Online] Sony. Available at: https://youtu.be/jjwG4rknlxw

Khaki, E. F. and Aidan, S. A. (2022). As Refugee Law Practitioners, We Oppose Canada's Double Standards. *The Maple.* Available at: www.readthemaple.com/as-refugee-law-practitioners-we-oppose-canadas-double-standards/

PEW Research Center. (2017). *U.S. muslims concerned about their place in society, but continue to believe in the American dream.* [Online] U.S.: PEW, 194 pages. Available at: www.pewresearch.org/religion/2017/07/26/identity-assimilation-and-community/

Tweenies/Zonneveld, Z, J. Bjorklund (2002). *Hip Hip Hooray.* [Online] BBC Music. Available at: https://youtu.be/wED8CQecqqk

# Recommended further reading

1.  Mernissi, F., (1992). *The Veil and the Male Elite*. New York: Perseus Books Publishing.

2.  Jebara, M., (2021). *Muhammad, the World-Changer: An intimate portrait*. New York: St. Martin's Essentials.

3.  Learn about water rationing and the many violations in the Occupied Territories of Palestine and Gaza—Makan, (2024). *Hub: Settlements*. [online] Available at: makan.org.uk

4.  Muslims for Progressive Values. (2019). *LGBTQI Resources*. [Online] Available at: www.mpvusa.org/lgbtqi-resources

# Index

www.ingramcontent.com/pod-product-compliance
Lightning Source LLC
Chambersburg PA
CBHW050340270326
41926CB00016B/3543